GETTING AWAY WITH
MURDER

GETTING AWAY WITH
MURDER

LENNY HAMILTON
WITH
CRAIG CABELL

JOHN BLAKE

Published by John Blake Publishing Ltd,
3 Bramber Court, 2 Bramber Road,
London W14 9PB, England

www.blake.co.uk

First published in hardback in 2006

ISBN-13: 978 1 84454 259 8
ISBN-10: 1 84454 259 9

British Library Cataloguing-in-Publication Data:

A catalogue record for this book is available from the British Library.

Design by www.envydesign.co.uk

Printed and bound in Great Britain by William Clowes Ltd, Beccles, Suffolk

1 3 5 7 9 10 8 6 4 2

Papers used by John Blake Publishing are natural, recyclable products made
from wood grown in sustainable forests. The manufacturing processes conform
to the environmental regulations of the country of origin.

All photographs from the authors' collection.

'I am 74 years of age at the time of writing, but if I had known then what I know now I would have gone and got a gun and shot that evil bastard Ronnie Kray because, just like every one of us, gangsters are not invincible. They too can die.'
LENNY HAMILTON

'Without courage there cannot be truth; and without truth there can be no other virtue.'
SIR WALTER SCOTT

'What it lies in our power to do, it lies in our power not to do.'
CHINESE PROVERB

ACKNOWLEDGEMENTS

I would like to thank all the people who have come forward to either talk to me about their experiences with the Krays or to be formerly interviewed for this book by Craig Cabell (the latter interviews are a formal back-up to some of the things I say in this book). I haven't mentioned every name here because some people still wish to remain anonymous. I would also like to thank the staff of the National Archive in Kew, who helped to maximise research time, and Eric and Jeff Mason for their time, friendship, Foreword and excellent photos.

I would also like to thank Leonard 'Nipper' Read, the brains behind the case against the Krays – surely one of the most sophisticated and successful pieces of policing this country has ever seen. Nipper and his team proved that crime doesn't pay. He also devoted some time to talk to me and to be interviewed for this book, thus adding substance to some of my findings. I would really like to thank him for that. He is a real gentleman. I won't forget his kindness.

I also owe a debt of gratitude to life-long friend of the Krays and all-round nice guy Laurie O'Leary for his time and kindness. Laurie has now passed on but his memory hasn't. Laurie was a smashing bloke. Never a gangster. He is a great loss to us all.

Thanks also to my great friends Billy Frost, George and Alan Dixon, plus all the other people that I call true friends and true men. God bless you all, especially those killed by the Twins, such as Jack McVitie, George Cornell, Frank Mitchell, Teddy Smith and the others who you will learn about in the pages of this book. God bless.

Finally, many thanks to my partner Gwen and daughter Katie, the two ladies I dedicate this book to.

LH, London 2006

CONTENTS

DRAMATIS PERSONAE

Abrahams, Harry
Former Kray gang member who left and formed his
own Firm.

Abrahams, Jean
Wife to Harry Abrahams.

Andrews, Jimmy
South London thief.

Bannister, Billy
Thief murdered by Kray twins.

Barrie, Ian
Kray Firm member who accompanied Ronnie into the Blind
Beggar pub as back-up man the night George Cornell was
shot dead.

Barry, Tony

Nightclub owner who was pressured into taking a gun to 'Blonde' Carol Skinner's house the night Jack McVitie was murdered and who was subsequently acquitted at trial.

Barry, John

Nightclub owner and brother to Tony.

Bender, Ronnie

Ex-soldier. Member of Kray Firm. Present at McVitie killing, but took no part in it; was given a 20-year sentence at Kray trial as a consequence.

Blasker (Doctor)

Quack doctor who supplied the Kray twins with medication.

Cater, Frank

Number Two to Nipper Read on the Kray case.

Cooper, Alan Bruce

Fraudster who worked alongside Krays and Leslie Payne.

Cornell, George

Thief and member of Richardson Firm. Shot dead by Ronnie Kray in the Blind Beggar pub.

Dickson, 'Scotch' Jack

Driver for Ronnie Kray. Drove Ronnie and Ian Barrie to Blind Beggar the night Ronnie killed Cornell. Was also one of Frank Mitchell's chaperones while he was in hiding from the authorities. Turned Queen's Evidence and was acquitted at the Kray trial.

Dixon, Alan
Brother of George.

Dixon, George
Had his own Firm with brother Alan before the Krays set up their own. Survived attempted murder by Ronnie Kray.

Donoghue, Albert
Former member of Harry Abrahams' Firm. Became member of Kray Firm when Abrahams was sentenced to five years' imprisonment. Became driver and money collector for Krays. Was shot in the foot by Reggie Kray. Turned Queen's Evidence at trial and was sentenced separately. Served two years.

Exley, Billy
Kray confidant until the Twins tried to kill him and threatened his family. Gave evidence at the trial and was acquitted.

Foreman, Freddie
Kray associate from South London. Was given ten years for his involvement in the disposal of Jack McVitie's body. He was also accused of being involved in the death of Frank Mitchell, but was acquitted.

Francis, Georgie
Grass, murdered by Reggie Kray.

Fraser, Frankie
Richardson Firm henchman. Tried to put an axe through Eric
Mason's head. Spent many years in prison.

Frost, Billy 'Jack'
Member of Kray Firm who disappeared at the same time as
'Mad' Teddy Smith. Wrongly believed to have been murdered
by the Krays.

Gerrard, Alfie
Member of Freddie Foreman's Firm.

Hamilton, Lenny
Ex-jewel thief who worked on Harry Abrahams' Firm before
becoming a driver for Alan Bruce Cooper. Was tortured with
red-hot pokers by Ronnie Kray.

Hart, Ronnie
Cousin of the Krays who was accused of assisting in the
murder of Jack McVitie. He was acquitted at trial.

Kray, Charlie (Snr)
Father to Charlie, Reggie and Ronnie Kray; husband to
Violet.

Kray, Charlie
Elder brother to Kray twins.

Kray, Dolly
First wife of Charlie Kray.

Kray, Reggie
Gangster and convicted murderer.

Kray, Ronnie
Gangster and convicted murderer.

Kray, Violet
Mother of Charlie, Reggie and Ronnie Kray and wife to Charlie Kray Snr.

Lambrianou, Chris
Brother of Tony. Present at McVitie's murder but played no part. Sentenced to 15 years imprisonment. Not a member of the Kray Firm.

Lambrianou, Tony
Would-be Kray Firm member. Played a role in McVitie murder and was sentenced to 15 years imprisonment. Many blame Tony for circumstances of McVitie's death.

Lisa (surname not known)
Hostess and sexual partner to Frank Mitchell while he was in hiding.

Mafia, Tony
Murdered, but not by the Kray twins as previously suspected.

Mason, Eric
Member of Kray Firm. Cut badly by Richardson gang and assaulted with axe by Frankie Fraser but never grassed.

McVitie, Jack 'the Hat'
Thief and member of the Kray Firm murdered by
Reggie Kray.

Mitchell, 'Mad' Frank (a.k.a. 'the Axeman')
Convict sprung from prison by Krays and murdered at
their request.

Morgan, Dickie
Friend of Krays who went on the run from the army
with them.

O'Leary, Laurie
Life-long friend of Krays but never a gangster.

Payne, Leslie 'the Brain'
Fraudster who worked for the Kray Firm.

Read, Leonard 'Nipper'
The man who successfully convicted the Krays.

The Rent Boy
Gay prostitute murdered by Ronnie Kray.

Richardson, Charlie
Firm leader from South London.

Richardson, Eddie
Firm leader from South London. Brother of
Charlie Richardson.

Scully, Brian
Thief murdered by Reggie Kray before Ronnie
killed Cornell.

Shea, Elsie
Mother of Frances and Frankie Shea.

Shea, Frances
First wife of Reggie Kray. Driven to suicide by the Twins.

Shea, Frank
Father of Frances and Frankie Shea.

Shea, Frankie
Brother of Frances Shea and the person Reggie Kray was
truly in love with.

Smith, 'Mad' Teddy
Playwright and member of the Kray Firm. Helped Frank
Mitchell escape from prison. Murdered by Reggie Kray.

Spot, Jack
Former gangster idolised by Ronnie Kray.

Squibb, Johnny
Life-long friend of Krays who assisted in a financial matter
concerning 'Peer and the Gangster' scam.

Stevenson, Melford
Judge at Kray trial.

The Undertaker (a.k.a. 'Kapo')
Polish gangster who cut up and disposed of bodies for the Twins.

Whitehead, Connie
Firm member. Present at the death of Jack McVitie but took no part in it. Was Ronnie's driver for a while but Ronnie ordered Connie's death towards the end when he believed that Connie was grassing to the police. Connie remained loyal and received eight years' imprisonment as a consequence.

FOREWORD

I had a nice surprise when I went to the Blind Beggar pub in Mile End. The first person I saw was an old pal of mine, Billy Frost. I hadn't seen Frostie for quite a few years, but as we got talking one of the first names that came up was Lenny Hamilton.

Frostie asked me to say a few words about Lenny as he had another book coming out. I knew it was bound to be an interesting tale that Lenny had to tell. Lenny and I led similar lives in the 1950s and 1960s, and if there was a jewel robbery, a wages snatch or a safe blown in those days it was a good bet that one of Lenny's mob was involved. Lenny worked with all the professionals, such as Harry Abrahams, and made a good living out of it. Like myself, he also managed to stay away from harming anyone.

I recently met up with Lenny and Frostie in the Beggar with my son, Jeff, and we had a few laughs over some of the stories about Ronnie Kray's mynah bird. I don't know if Lenny put that bird up to say 'Ronnie's a gangster, Ronnie's a gangster', but I know Ronnie didn't take it in fun. Lenny and Ronnie later had a big fall out, which is in Lenny's first book, but I know that Charlie Kray and Lenny were good friends.

Lenny Hamilton is well respected and I'm sure his book will be a great success. Everyone that used the 81 Club in Mile End could only say nice things about him. Good luck with your book, Lenny. I am adding my name to this book because I have the utmost respect for you.

Eric Mason
July 2006

INTRODUCTION

*'Nipper Read, when he came to see me in prison, said to me,
"Len, if you make a statement, other people will follow you."
And that's because I was well known in the East End.
Still am, I suppose. But they were Nipper Read's exact
words to me. I don't lie.'*

LENNY HAMILTON

I first met Lenny Hamilton while researching my book *The Kray Brothers – The Image Shattered*. What I quickly found was that some of Lenny's views were quite different from my own. He had written his own well-received book, *Branded By Ronnie Kray*, and had appeared on several documentaries concerning the Twins. What I admired most about him was the fact that he was one of the few people who actually verbally castigated the Twins on TV while they were still alive.

After my book was released – and well received – Lenny got in touch with me. He was most interested in my analysis of the Kray murders, not just the highly publicised killings of George Cornell and Jack 'the Hat' McVitie, but up to seven other murders.

Seven murders? Yes. Lenny also believed the figure was seven. That's why he called me. We swapped notes and found that we agreed on many issues connected to other murders not usually attributed to the Twins. These issues had never previously been put before the public. Suddenly, we had an exciting topic on our hands. After several talks Lenny and I found that if we put our heads together we could add substance to the claims of these other murders and shed further light on the Krays. This was groundbreaking stuff and, most of all, we had first-hand interviews with people who had never come forward before, major players, and we also had official documentation from the National Archive that both Lenny and I had studied.

When I look back over the many interviews I have completed it reads like a list of heavyweight known names. These aren't fringe figures but substantial characters such as Charlie Kray, Billy 'Jack' Frost, Laurie O'Leary, Leonard 'Nipper' Reed and Eric Mason. These men really knew the Twins and their antics.

Really, though, this is Lenny's book. It relies heavily on his first-hand information and perception, as you will see. Lenny organised many meetings with people – some of whom still do not wish to be named in connection with the Twins, as if their knowledge would still somehow get them in trouble. Such is the fear instilled by the Krays to this day.

Some people will ask how much of this book was written by Lenny and how much by me. Put simply, Lenny provided the whole narrative in long hand and I typed it up adding dates and other unambiguous facts. I then conducted independent interviews with key people to add weight to Lenny's memories, then went back to the National Archive to rationalise certain key facts and provide factual details concerning the deaths of George Cornell and Jack McVitie, which Lenny had no first-hand knowledge of. This approach has, we believe, created a more rounded picture of events than any other book about the Krays that has appeared so far.

For example, when one reads John Pearson's very well received *Profession Of Violence*, he is quoted as saying that Billy Frost had disappeared at the same time as Teddy Smith and was presumed dead. This is no criticism of Mr Pearson's work. When *The Profession Of Violence* was originally released Frost was still in hiding and Mr Pearson was simply quoting the suspicions of the police at that time. Billy Frost, or Frostie, is now back in circulation. He's an amazing character and he provided me with an illuminating interview while attending a reunion with Lenny and Eric Mason.

Most people connected with the Krays are now in their mid-to-late 70s. Frankly, they want to enjoy the rest of their lives away from the influence of the infamous Twins, but they also know that there is an obligation on them to tell their Kray story. I want it known that none of them asked for any money for their part in this book and that they came forward to support Lenny and assist in telling the truth about the Krays.

At this juncture, both Lenny and I would like to express our heartfelt thanks to Laurie O'Leary (who helped me so much with *The Image Shattered*), whose assistance in both our personal and public lives has been enormous. Laurie wrote his own respected book concerning his life-long friend Ronnie Kray, which must go down as one of the most important books concerning the Twins, written from the exclusive viewpoint of a friend. Laurie was never on the wrong side of the law and indeed assisted Lenny when his daughter needed some work experience a few years back. He was a raconteur and knew his wine. I have fond memories of chatting with him in his Thameside office in Wapping, drinking Bordeaux or tea with him and his lovely wife in his beautiful house in the East End. Laurie sadly died recently and Lenny and I would like to thank him and acknowledge his memory.

The Kray Twins were the most wicked gangsters Britain has ever seen. They slashed and killed without mercy. When I first interviewed Nipper Reed he started the conversation by stating: 'You youngsters don't know what they were like.' Fortunately, I did. I had spoken to members of the Kray Firm, their friends and associates. Now, with the help of Lenny Hamilton, the untold story of the Twins' evil reign can be told in its full gory detail. As Lenny says: 'Every word is the truth.'

Perhaps now people will begin to understand why the Twins never received the parole they so craved. If I left any unanswered questions at the end of my last book then this volume holds all the answers. Lenny feels the same way. It is due to him that this book has seen the light of day in the first place, and I thank him and his East End friends and associates for allowing me to play my own small part in it. I believe in what Lenny says here. When I spoke to Nipper Read about Lenny he could only say good things about him. I know that shortly after I spoke to Mr Read Lenny spoke to him, too. I know this because I provided the contact on Read's say so. What you have here is the only book of its kind on the Krays – one where many different people have come together from both sides of the law to agree on many untold or little-known stories about the Twins. When Charlie Kray once said to me that he disliked the movie *The Krays*, telling me 'I could have given them a story they wouldn't believe,' he was hinting at things about the Twins that were not publicly known. The reminiscences of the Krays laid down here are pretty close to the fantastical story that Charlie was alluding to.

One last thing. Nipper Read explained to me that Lenny was most important in bringing the Krays to trial. Although he was a criminal himself, Lenny knew that the Twins had to be stopped. He was under the real threat of death for talking to Nipper Read about the Twins' criminal activities and death threats were passed on to his wife and children too. On this basis it is right that Lenny, along with his late friend Billy Exley, are recognised for their part in bringing the Krays to justice. As Lenny himself once told me of his part in the Kray trial: 'When I had finished giving my evidence, the Old Bill punched the air because they knew that they had got the committal to the Old Bailey from my evidence.' The Twins had gone too far, so it was left to people like Lenny to put the record straight.

And he's still doing it now.

Craig Cabell
London, July 2006

PROLOGUE

I was born in the Commercial Road, Stepney, in 1931. I was brought up with my family in Ely Terrace, a turning off White Horse Lane, within a tight-knit Jewish community.

During the nineteenth century it was the Jews who opened many factories around the Aldgate and Whitechapel areas, mostly making clothing. The Jewish tailor shops were well respected and both men and women went there if they wanted a hand-made suit. It was an area where everyone knew the importance and value of hard work – especially as work was so difficult to come by. Even the dockers, who worked in the Royal London Docks, were finding life difficult in the 1930s. They turned up at the docks every day but were not guaranteed a day's work. And no work meant no pay.

It was a hard life for everyone in those days, especially the East End housewives. Their constant worry was how they were going to feed and clothe their children. Every wife or mother became an expert at creative accounting or lateral thinking in order to try and battle through their lives. Most goods were bought on tick, so families were always struggling to keep up the payments on the things that they had already bought, as well as find money to buy the extra things in life that they needed in the future too.

I lived with my mum and dad and four brothers and three sisters. Being the youngest son, I had to wear all my elder brothers' cast offs. When one of my socks got a hole in the heel my mother would turn it round so that the toe part became the heel.

The East End was a tight-knit community all right. Everybody knew everybody else and neighbours would always try and help each other out. We were all in the same boat. However, I don't see that same community spirit nowadays. As the standard of living has improved, the camaraderie between people has waned. Back in the 1930s the Jewish people had Oswald Mosley's Black Shirts to contend with. This mini-Hitler and his troops smashed windows as they marched down the streets of the East End. I recall an up-and-coming gangster at that time, a Jew by the name of Jack Comer – more famously known by his nickname of Jack Spot. Jack stood up against Mosley and his Black Shirts. He faced them with his own group of hard men and ran them off the streets on 4 October 1936. What was known as the Battle of Cable Street became very famous and enhanced Jack's image across London.

There were other famous gangs around. The Sabini brothers were very active in the East End up until the outbreak of WWII, and the Italians had their own Little Italy working out of Clerkenwell. But above all, Jack Spot became known as the King of the Underworld. Jack became an icon among many

Jews and Jewish followers. His success increased throughout the 1940s and 1950s, running a lot of prostitution and other rackets in the West End. He also did well at the races.

As I reminisce about the old East End, it seems to me that I am living in another world now. It's not the same place. There are more ethnic minorities and mosques are popping up everywhere – it is not the place I grew up knowing. People have died or moved on and the atmosphere has changed. In my day old people were not beaten up on the street by youths, yet I was recently attacked while getting a bus home. I'm 74 years of age at the time of writing.

So, forgive me if I talk about the good old days – even if it was in the good old days that I was burned with red-hot pokers by Ronnie Kray. After all, that's why you have picked up this book. You want to know about the most evil side of the Kray twins. There have been many books and television shows concerning those two, but rarely has the full truth been told.

I knew the Twins for more than 50 years. And I know that a lot of what has been said about them during that time is at best only half true, if not completely false. I was one of a handful of people prepared to castigate them on national TV when they were alive and I will go on criticising them until the day I die, because I knew what they were really like. I've been no angel myself. I was a jewel thief. But what those two did was far worse. They cut, slashed, terrorised and murdered so many people.

It wasn't just Jack McVitie and George Cornell that they killed. There was Frank Mitchell and Teddy Smith, too. Most criminologists know about Mitchell and Smith, but few know about my old friend Brian Scully and another old friend of mine called Billy. Tears come to my eyes every time I think of Brian and Billy. I could have helped save them, especially Billy. It tears me apart just to think of him. You see, the Krays haunt me. They may be dead but they are not forgotten. They physically and mentally tortured me.

Other people in the East End can't forget or forgive them either. Does the public know the truth behind the death of Frances Shea, Reggie's wife? Well, I know Frances' brother Frankie and you'll find out the truth about that poor girl's death in this book. But there was even more hurt. What about the poor old bank manager who hanged himself because of the Kray gang? Whoever mentioned him before? And here you see a pattern: two people taking their own lives because of the terror instilled in them by the Krays. That's not all. Nipper Read told me of one Kray witness that he was taking for questioning. She thought that she was being kidnapped by the Krays and tried to escape by jumping out of the car and into the Thames. She wasn't the only one who tried to commit suicide before giving evidence against the Twins at their trial, as you will learn.

You may ask yourself why these facts haven't been mentioned before? The reason is quite simple: Nipper Read did enough to put the Kray twins away for the rest of their lives and the people of the East End, the ones who really knew the Krays, never felt the need to say much more than what the local newspapers and youngsters wished to know. But when I look at the East End of today and still see tributes and respect for the Krays it makes me sick. That is why I have written this book, to show the depths of evil the Kray twins went to during their reign of terror. This is the East End's story of the Krays. The area they said they loved, but terrorised so viciously. What you read here comes direct from the people who *really* knew them. People like Eric Mason, Billy Frost and myself. We were there. We remember. How could we forget?

They say memories fade but the scars still linger. Well, I'm here to tell you that in my case both the scars *and* the memories linger.

Let me begin by giving you a bit of background on the Twins, where they came from and how they became so bad. I do this to put the rest of this book into perspective and to give people my point of view as someone who grew up in the East End and who had a fleeting association with the Twins. I won't lie to you.

Violet Kray gave birth to identical twin boys on 24 October 1933 and she named them Reginald and Ronald. At the time she was living in Stean Street [(1)], off the Kingsland Road, which, strictly speaking is more North London than East End. Violet was a lovely woman and a very good mother who doted on her boys. She never had a bad word to say about them until the day she passed away. There was another child, elder brother Charlie who was named after his father. He grew up to be a good man.

Violet felt very isolated living in Stean Street, especially as her husband Charlie was away most of the time working on the knocker to buy old gold and silver. He travelled the country doing this but even when he was home Violet saw very little of him as he would spend his free time drinking in the local pubs. Charlie Jnr., six years older than the Twins, was Violet's only real company. So, when one day a house became vacant in Vallance Road in Bethnal Green – the street where Violet's father and two sisters lived – she jumped at the chance to take it and quickly moved in. She was over the moon to be living next door to her family. This was the house that would come to be known as Fort Vallance once the Twins' criminal careers got underway.

The trouble began in their teenage years. Violet, indulgent of her two boys, didn't really do anything to keep them in check. Nor did Charlie Jnr., fair haired and laid back like his mother, crack down on his brothers' increasingly disruptive behaviour. The Twins were much more like their father in looks and temperament – dark-haired and aggressive. Unfortunately, Charlie Snr. was either not around enough or interested enough to discipline Ronnie and Reggie either, not that he would eventually stand much chance.

After WWII Charlie Jnr. joined the navy and became a boxing champion. He also set up a gym at home where his brothers could practise the sport. They soon became very good boxers, and that's when bad things started to happen. Taking their boxing skills out onto the streets, the Twins began to get into all sorts of scraps throughout their early teens.

My first run-in with them came a few years after this.

I was coming home from work one day. I saw this big chap fighting with two young boys, so I got stuck in to give them some help. In doing so I helped them to get away. To my surprise, the man Ronnie and Reggie were fighting with was a plain-clothes police officer from Arbour Square Police Station who was trying to arrest them for being on the run from the army [2]. Although they got away on this occasion – with my help – the army did eventually catch up with them and they served some time in Shepton Mallet Prison before being kicked out of the armed forces completely [3].

A little while after this I was in the Regal Snooker Hall in Eric Street, just off Mile End Road, having a game of snooker with one of my mates. A chap tapped me on the shoulder and when I turned around I didn't recognise him. He said: 'You don't know me but I'm Reggie Kray and this is my brother, Ronnie. Thanks for helping us out that time with the Old Bill.' When I got a good look at his brother I thought I was seeing double, because they were identical [4]. After shaking hands we went across the road to the Wentworth pub and had a few drinks. During the conversation they asked me if I used the snooker club regularly. I said I did. Then they asked me if it was very busy. I told them that the place was a piss-hole with only a few decent tables in it. They left shortly after that and I returned to the snooker hall. When I got back blokes were coming up to me and asking how long I had known the Twins. I could not believe that they were really that popular.

I stopped using the snooker hall soon after this as fights kept breaking out in there and a group of hooligans began coming in and ripping up the tables. A couple of months later I was in the Poplar Dance Hall one Saturday night when a boy I knew called Patsy came over and asked why I never went to the snooker hall anymore. When I told him it was because of all the trouble, he replied that the place had now been cleaned up and that the troublemakers had been sorted out by the club's new owners – the Krays. Being curious, the next afternoon I went round to the hall and to my surprise the

13

whole place had been redecorated. It had a lovely clean tea bar with my old mate Dickie Moughton running it. It was a transformation.

I got talking to Dickie to find out how the Twins had taken over the hall. He told me that some boys from the Kray gang had been sent round over the course of a few weeks to have mock fights and frighten punters away. Once the place had been turned into a ghost town the Krays stepped in and bought it for a song. Within a few months the Regal Snooker Hall became a little gold mine to the Twins, and word soon got around about its success.

Enter the Maltese.

A gang of Maltese gangsters that worked in the West End heard about the snooker hall and decided to muscle in. One day, my mate Dickie was in the tea bar with the Krays when half a dozen of these gangsters came into the hall and demanded to see the governors. Reggie was standing by one of the tables while Ronnie was up at the bar on the phone. Ronnie shouted: 'Me and my brother are the governors, what do you want?' One of the Maltese stepped forward, placing a hand on the side of the snooker table where Reggie was standing. He said: 'For 25 per cent of the takings we'll keep trouble out of here.' Ronnie replied: 'We don't need cunts like you, we can look after ourselves.' Quick as a flash, Reggie produced a knife and stabbed the guy next to him through the hand. Ronnie then pulled out a sword from behind the bar and took on the rest of the gang, chasing them out of the hall and cutting a few along the way. When Ronnie returned, he went up to the one Reggie had pinned to the table with his knife and slashed the man's arse with his sword. From that day forward they never had any more trouble with rivals. The rise of the Kray empire had begun [5].

In 1956 Ronnie Kray was sentenced to three years in prison for wounding with intent and possession of an offensive weapon [6]. In the meantime Reggie and Charlie opened a drinking club in Bow Road and called it the Double R. It was furnished in a very high-class style and attracted many of the top celebrities of the time. It was as if the West End had come to the East End and Reggie and 'Champagne' Charlie (as the elder Kray brother came to be known) were enjoying every minute of it [7]. That was until Ronnie Kray came out of prison.

Ronnie was mentally unbalanced and if anyone looked at him in the wrong way he would have a go at them. Once he became involved in the club he caused many fights and took money from the till to give away or spend. People started to stay away from the place in their droves. The takings dropped and then the police finally had the premises closed down [8].

However, the Twins were not ruined. They still had money coming in from their protection rackets and long firm frauds, set up by a man named Leslie Payne. By this time almost everybody in the East End was terrified of the Krays. We all knew that Ronnie Kray was homosexual and a paranoid schizophrenic. I also knew that Reggie Kray was bisexual. In 1960 I saw him with my own eyes having sex with a young boy at a party. The East End had had its fair share of villains in the past but the Krays were thugs the likes of which no one had seen before or since.

After the Double R, the Krays soon opened another club

in the Mile End Road, which they named the Kentucky. One of the little scams they ran there were the so-called charity nights. The first of these was for the nurses from Bankcroft Hospital in Mile End. Billy Daniels, who'd had a hit with 'That Old Black Magic', was the star turn and I was helping out behind the bar.

It was a very good night, with thousands of pounds taken for charity. The Lord Mayor and Mayoress of Stepney were the last members of the public to leave, after which myself, Harry Abrahams, Ronnie, Reggie and Charlie Kray remained in the club. When all the money was finally counted up, two thirds of it went to the Krays and the other third went to the nurses. The Krays never did anything for nothing.

It was around this time that their gang became known as the Firm. Things were getting serious. Not only that, Ronnie was becoming more violent. He was popping pills left, right and centre to control his schizophrenia. And it was not just Ronnie that was acting up; Reggie was prone to a bit of odd behaviour, too – as I witnessed when I went round to Vallance Road the day after the so-called charity night. Mrs Kray opened the door and showed me into the living room where Reggie and Charlie were seated. They thanked me for helping them out in the club the night before and gave me £50 for my trouble. Then Mrs Kray came in with tea and a plate full of sandwiches for us. It was then that I saw Reggie go a bit funny, holding his head in both hands. When he took his hands away from his head he said to Charlie: 'Ronnie's been hurt.'

'Look Reggie,' Charlie replied, 'Ronnie isn't here.' I just sat there not knowing what to do and thinking to myself that

Reggie must be going mad. That was until the phone rang and Charlie took the call. His face went white and he told Reggie that Ronnie had got himself a bit pissed and had fallen down the stairs in a pub. He had put his shoulder out and had been taken to the London Hospital. That night, Harry Abrahams and I went to the Kentucky Club to have a drink and to find out how Ronnie was. When we got inside we saw the three brothers at the end of the bar with Bobby Ramsey, Doughie King and Limehouse Willy. Harry asked Ronnie if he was OK and Ronnie said that as he was coming down the stairs a black cat got under his feet and caused him to fall. He then said that if he ever got his hands on that cat he would wring its fucking neck! Of course, we all burst out laughing because, to tell you the truth, Ronnie Kray had a very good sense of humour [9].

The Kray Firm grew quickly and they became a force to be reckoned with. By this time they had hurt quite a lot of people, too. They were getting away with their crimes because of the fear they generated in the East End. I, for one, was scared of them, but I was not alone. Ronnie Kray in particular always wanted to be a gangster and he really did think he was another Al Capone. To look like gangsters, the Twins switched from having their suits made by Woods – their tailor in Kingsland Road – to the more upmarket tailors of Savile Row. Even their shoes and shirts were handmade for them.

However, despite the fact that they dressed the same you could by now tell the Twins apart. Because of all the pills he was taking, Ronnie had become bloated. He also brushed his hair down flat with Brylcreem, which made him look a lot more menacing.

So this is what the Krays were like as they began their infamous rise. There are plenty more tales to tell about their early days, and I would like to share a few more of them here in order to build up a complete picture of what the Twins were like before they went on to commit the major crimes for which they would become notorious – and before the murders which are being revealed here for the first time.

Before Ronnie went to prison to serve his three years, he and Reggie went to see a second-hand car dealer in the Mile End Road. They were after protection money, and when the car dealer refused to pay, Ronnie shot him in the leg. Unsurprisingly, this persuaded the car dealer to change his mind (as did the Twins' revelation that they knew all about their victim's shady dealings in the second-hand car trade that would stop him from going to the police). With the protection deal agreed, the Twins arranged for a character called Dr Blasker to treat the car dealer's injuries. Blasker was a struck-off physician who helped out the Krays from time to time, patching up their victims and supplying Ronnie with the pills that he became so dependent on.

Blasker was a heavy gambler and drinker and was often seen around the illegal gambling clubs in the East End. I suppose he did the odd job for the Krays to fuel his addictions. I say this because he did a good job on my face when, years later, Ronnie burnt me with red-hot pokers. Because of that, I always gave Blasker a few quid when I saw him in any of the gambling clubs. Blasker wasn't a bad man. He was just as scared of the Twins as the rest of us.

The Regency Club was in Amhurst Road, Hackney. It had a large upstairs bar and a nice stage where, as well as resident singers, people used to get up from the audience and deliver a song or two. Later on, they also opened up a Chinese restaurant in there. The club was run by the four Barry brothers and not the Kray twins, as is sometimes said. The Twins' only interest in the place was the protection money they drew from the Barrys.

The Regency was a popular venue and people came from all over London to enjoy themselves there. The Barrys were nice people and helped out a lot of people over the years. Unlike the Twins, they did not advertise who they helped out; they did it because they had good hearts. However, because of the Kray connection the police finally closed the club down and the Barrys had their livelihood taken away from them. This was just one of the many different ways in which the Krays managed to ruin other people's lives.

By this time the Twins were getting protection money from publicans, drinking clubs and shop-keepers from all over the East End. To be honest, some people did go to the Twins voluntarily to ask for protection – but many more had the Twins' offer of protection forced upon them.

I have mentioned Leslie Payne. He was very important to the Krays. When he was brought onto the Firm the serious money started to roll in. He was a very clever man. It was Payne who introduced them to the Long Firm Frauds and it was due to Payne that they also got control of high class clubs such as Esmeralda's Barn in Knightsbridge and the Cambridge Rooms on Kingston by-pass.

A lot of celebrities and people with political connections

started to gather around the Krays at that time. The Twins loved it and started to have their most famous photos taken with all these influential people. This celebrity socialising continued until one night when a fight broke out between two people on the Firm, resulting in one of them being cut very badly. That was when the dodgy side of the Krays was seen at first-hand by the influential mob and they didn't like it at all. They started to drift away, and at the same time the police began to show more and more interest in the Krays' activities. In many ways, it was the beginning of the end.

The police certainly had enough to look into. There was the long firm frauds, the protection rackets, the partial work for charity, the GBH and general violence and enforcement that they routinely dished out. Then, of course, there were the murders. Ultimately, it was the murders that brought down the Krays – and the reason why they were never granted parole during their 30-year sentences. This book will look at those murders in detail. It will begin with the Kray trial and the murders for which the Twins were known, and will then go on to explain the more obscure killings perpetrated by the Krays, explaining why they have never before been publicised – until now.

Lenny Hamilton

CHAPTER 1

THE KRAY TRIAL

'Those lips that Love's own hand did make Breath'd forth the
sound that said, "I hate",'
WILLIAM SHAKESPEARE

It was the greatest show trial of the 20th century. More glamorous than that of the Great Train Robbers or the Knight brothers' bullion job. This was the feared Kray twins. They had been in the dock before. Leonard 'Nipper' Read had already had a shot at putting them away; but they had slipped through his fingers on that occasion. But that was nearly five years ago [10]. It was now 1969 and Read had learned by his mistakes. He now had a crack team working on the Krays, monitoring their activities, compiling evidence and persuading witnesses to come forward. Special privileges had been extended to Read and his squad to ensure that they could give their full attention to convicting the Krays.

The case had to be watertight. Why? Because the Krays

were getting more and more powerful. They weren't just big in the criminal underworld; they were moving in exalted social circles, too. Influential people were beginning to be associated with them. Even Lord Boothby had officially spoken on their behalf. It was time to take them down.

Of course, there was more to Boothby's support of the Twins than met the eye. For one, there was the famous photograph of the 'peer and the gangster' that appeared in a tabloid, which showed that Boothby moved in criminal circles. The photograph was said to have been taken by 'Mad' Teddy Smith, a known homosexual [11], which added another layer of scandal to the story. According to police records in the National Archive, one Johnny Squibb [12] was paid by the newspapers for providing the picture. Squibb was a friend of the Krays, so it's not unreasonable to assume that the Twins played some part in the process. Boothby, it seems, was under scrutiny – from the Twins. What would that lead to and what else, if anything, did the Krays have on Boothby? If we believe John Pearson's account in *The Cult Of Violence*, Boothby had a fondness for adolescent boys and gay parties [13].

And it was not just Boothby that the Krays could take down [14]. Once they became a real threat to the Establishment Ronnie and Reggie had to be stopped before they became unmanageable.

Enter Nipper Read for his second crack at them.

This time he spread his net wide. He gathered intelligence and made some tough decisions. One thing he discovered was that the extent of the Krays' crimes was a lot bigger than many people imagined. 'They were murdering people willy-nilly,' he explained in 2001 [15]. But as the investigation wore on it became clear that there were only two murders that the Twins could be held fully accountable for and in which the case against them was secure. It was decided to focus on these two murders in order to secure convictions against Ronnie and Reggie Kray. The aim was to show that Ronnie murdered George Cornell and that Reggie in turn killed Jack 'the Hat' McVitie – with each brother urging the other on. It was a calculated gamble by Nipper Read, and it paid off.

Lord Widgery, Lord Chief Justice at the Krays' appeal on 22 July 1969, proved that Read's approach was justified, when he ruled that:

These two cases exhibit unusual features in common; each was committed in cold blood and without obvious motivation. Each bore the stamp of a gang leader asserting his authority by killing in the presence of witnesses, whose silence could be assured by that authority. Neither murder could be committed except on the basis that members of the Firm would rally round and clear up the traces and secure the silence of those who may be inclined to give the offenders away. All these factors make it important and desirable in the public interest for these two unusual cases to be tried together. Also, the interest of the press in this affair was so great that if the two murders had been tried separately the publicity attending the first trial would have made a fair trial on the remaining charges impossible.

By focusing on just two murders the police were able to bring down the mighty Kray twins, who were sentenced to *at least*

30 years each. A by-product of this approach was that all of their other crimes seemed to be forgotten in the wake of the Cornell and McVitie convictions. There was no mention, for example, of the rent boy that Ronnie Kray murdered after he refused him sex. Nothing was said either about Teddy Smith, who disappeared one day like Lord Lucan, never to return, and nor was Brian Scully's death mentioned.

It was clearly a tough decision that Nipper Read had to take, but it was a necessary one. There was evidence and there were witnesses for both the Cornell and McVitie cases – something that could not be said for the other murders of which the Twins were suspected. This being so, the police had to focus their attentions on the things they could clearly prove and not confuse the jury with the details of other crimes, especially murders for which the evidence was not forthcoming.

According to his book, *The Man Who Nicked The Krays*, Nipper Read held the pre-arrest briefing in the early hours of 7 May 1968. At 6:00 a.m. that morning he made his move. At various addresses around London doors were simultaneously kicked in as the police arrested the Krays and their associates. Everything went smoothly. Algie Hemingway jemmied open the front door of the Twins' mother's flat and Read and his officers ran inside. Within seconds the Twins had been arrested and cuffed.

Nipper Read has told me that on their arrest the Twins were quite arrogant. They'd been arrested before and had got away with it and thought that they would this time, too. How wrong they were. Nipper Read had done his homework. He knew that members of the Firm were now prepared to turn against Ronnie and Reggie. He also knew that members of the public were ready to stand up and be counted as well, including the barmaid of the Blind Beggar pub who witnessed Ronnie kill George Cornell, and Lisa, the girl who supplied sexual favours to Frank Mitchell after his jailbreak.

There were so many offences levelled against the Twins that it took 36 hours to write up the charge sheets. Consequently, they were not finally charged until the early hours of 10 May. At this stage they were held accountable for two cases of conspiracy to murder, two cases of blackmail, six cases relating to stolen bonds, four long firm frauds and one GBH charge – this last one pertaining to a certain branding with red-hot pokers by Ronnie Kray.

The Krays were packed off to one prison while various members of the Firm were dispersed to other jails around the country. Meanwhile, witnesses were put in safe houses with 24-hour police protection. For Nipper Read this was a very trying time, with little sleep and a lot of pressure. No trial like this had ever been planned before. It would be almost impossible to pull off something similar today.

It took a good few months for the committals to be made and during that time more people came forward to give evidence against the Twins, such as Lenny 'Brooks' Dunn, in whose flat Frank Mitchell was harboured. However, the poor man was so scared of what he was getting himself into that he almost succeeded in committing suicide (see Chapter 2). Dunn's behaviour was extreme but not unusual. Most of the witnesses in the case were paranoid and in fear for their safety as the Firm's reputation for violence extended beyond the prison walls that held its members. However, by 22 October the committals had been executed and the build-up to the trial itself began in earnest.

All of this hard work and activity came to a head on Wednesday, 8 January 1969, when the Kray trial opened in No. 1 Court of the Old Bailey. Ronnie and Reggie were 35 years old. Their brother Charlie stood in the dock alongside them, as did seven of their associates: John 'Ian' Barrie, Tony Lambrianou, Chris Lambrianou, Ronnie Bender, Connie Whitehead, Tony Barry and Freddie Foreman.

The courtroom itself was packed, not least with a host of news-hungry media. With ten defendants crammed into the dock the presiding judge, Mr Justice Melford Stevenson, set the no-nonsense tone of the trial by issuing the humiliating decree that each of the accused would be forced to wear a numbered placard around his neck. He thought it would be easier to identify who was who in the dock! [16] Unsurprisingly, the Krays' barrister, John Platts-Mills, opposed this ruling. Led by Ronnie, the defendants refused to wear their identification numbers – all accept Tony Barry, who kept his on throughout the trial and who was later acquitted.

The trial itself did not go the way the Twins wanted it to. As the pressure mounted tempers began to fray. At one point Ronnie Kray went in the dock and quite frankly embarrassed himself, calling the prosecuting counsel a 'fat slob'. Here was the most feared gangster in England resorting to petty name calling [17].

Then, on 8 March 1969, after a three-day summing up, the jury reached their verdict. The sentences were particularly heavy: Ronnie and Reggie Kray were handed 30 years each; Charlie Kray got 10 years; John Barrie, 20 years; Ronnie

Bender, 20 years; Tony Lambrianou, 15 years; Chris Lambrianou, 15 years; Connie Whitehead, 8 years; Freddie Foreman, 10 years. These sentences were the highest ever given at the Old Bailey, totalling 160 years (if one takes into consideration the two years given to Albert Donoghue, who was tried separately).

Justice, it seemed, had been done. But the full extent of the Krays' crimes had not been exposed before the court and the media. A further trial for the murder of Frank Mitchell would take place from 15 April 1969 (see Chapter 2) and Read would attempt to try the Twins further on other charges (see Nipper Read interview at Annexe of this book for confirmation). But these further prosecutions never really got off the ground and the taxpayer was saved a lot of money. It was generally agreed that 30 years was punishment enough and that the Twins were unlikely to taste freedom again anytime soon.

Yet while all this is true, and despite the constant pushing on the part of Nipper Read for more convictions, it's still the case that the Twins had got away with murder.

The Kray trial and the murders of George Cornell and Jack McVitie are still fascinating subjects today, almost 40 years after the final sentence was passed and years after the Twins and their elder brother have passed away. Part of this fascination lies as much in what we don't know as what we do know. What other crimes did the Twins commit? Why were they never granted parole? And, the million dollar question – who else did they kill?

Even Reggie Kray towards the end of his life seemed

unsure as to just how many murders he had committed. In an interview conducted as he lay on his deathbed Reggie hesitated before admitting to one further killing to go with his McVitie conviction. One plausible explanation for this hesitation is that Reggie was preparing to admit to even more murders than this new one. He didn't, but that may be as much to do with the booze- and tranquilliser-induced state that Reggie Kray was in at the time than anything else. Perhaps he simply could not remember.

But, as had already been pointed out, the decision had been made long before to try the Twins for just two murders – no matter what.

Before the trial, Reggie Kray admitted to being depressed. His wife had committed suicide and he had fallen down a slippery slope since. He didn't know what he was doing. If this was the case, and it may well have been, how was it that he was not allowed to claim diminished responsibility? Surely that would have helped him. Is it unreasonable to claim that the police and the legal system decided to fight fire with fire when it came to the Twins and make sure that they were convicted and put away forever?

If this sounds like a conspiracy theory it should be remembered that, as Tony Lambrianou told Craig Cabell whilst researching *The Kray Brothers – The Image Shattered*: 'Freddie Foreman came in with a slip of paper with some numbers on. This was before sentence was passed. And those numbers we eventually found corresponded with the sentences we would all eventually get.'

Yes, the Krays were bad, and in this situation the police and the legal system had to do what it had to do to get them. This was especially true of Nipper Read. If he didn't get the Krays they would get him. There was a bounty on his head. He explains: 'There was a contract on me for £20,000, which was a lot of money in those days.'

This all helps to explain why certain crimes were never mentioned at the trial, and why the sentences handed down were so harsh – and why, as insinuated by Tony Lambrianou, the outcome of the trial was so contrived. Leslie Payne provided a 200-page document detailing the Twins' fraudulent dealings in detail. He turned against the Twins when Jack McVitie was sent to kill him. Nipper Read was told, in effect, that the Twins had gone down for life and that there was no point in further trying them when there was no possibility of extending the 30-year sentences they had been given.

Society was scared of the Krays. 'Nobody is ever going to get as big as you again,' Charlie Kray was told at the time [18]. Indeed, Reggie Kray said a similar thing himself when he admitted: 'The police did their job well – they knew they had one chance and they took it. If they had failed the Krays would have been as unbreakable as we thought we were.'

So there you have it. Everyone agreed that the Krays had gone too far and had to be stopped – by any means necessary.

With the passing of time the Kray trial has become the 'official version' of events, with few people questioning what the Twins really got up to – especially as the Krays' image has been so softened and romanticised over the years. The idea that Ronnie and Reggie were much worse than we have previously been led to believe is possibly hard to accept, but it is true nonetheless.

And while the true story of the Krays struggles to be

known there is no shortage of more unusual theories about why the Twins were treated as they were by the law. There are some people in the East End, for instance, who maintain that a secret international society could have been behind the Kray trial. All this sort of thing does is keep alive the Kray myth and obscures the truth. This is why this book focuses on documenting the words of people who were there at the time, who knew the Krays and who worked with them or investigated them.

This book also reveals or revives stories that were not used at the Kray trial at the time. Take the story of Billy Frost, for example. In Nipper Read's book on the Krays he stated that Billy 'Jack' Frost, one time driver of the Krays, was not called to give evidence against the Twins at the trial because his role in the Firm was not as central as that of some other witnesses. This meant that the defence could have portrayed him as a peripheral figure to the Kray organisation and thus put doubt in the jury's mind about his evidence.

Also, Billy Frost could probably have better been used to offer information about other Kray crimes, not necessarily the murders of Cornell and McVitie, which would have made the case more complex. Frostie, like Billy Exley, knew the Krays well. He was a confidant – and there weren't many of those on the Kray Firm. He even stayed with the Twins for a time away from Vallance Road and heard them plotting with each other throughout the night on a regular basis. He truly *was* their confidant.

Billy Frost's story is one of the last untold tales of the Kray Firm. But his story didn't sit well with the angle that Nipper Read was building for trial so it was not used. This shows that

Nipper Read left nothing to chance or criticism. He focused everything on the two murders to the exclusion of all else. He had to remain focused. Why? Because if he brought too much other evidence in, the case would become more complex; and if the case became more complex, the Twins couldn't be tried for the same murder and there was a risk that one or both of them would be acquitted.

What all of this does mean is that the damning evidence that wasn't or could not be used *then* can be revealed *now*.

Now that we know why the trial took on the shape that it did we can begin to add to it the stories of those who were barred from taking part – or who did not want to take part. By adding these new testimonies to known and accepted fact we can create a more full and intricate picture of Britain's most infamous gangsters [19]. The main reason why public opinion is divided over the Krays is because the full extent of their penchant for killing has not been exposed before. The odd thing is that, when the people who knew them get together and talk, it is amazing to find that they all agree on the same issues, and those issues cut deep. Very deep. The trial only scraped the surface of the Kray twins' murdering ways. There were most definitely other murders.

When one talks about the Kray trial, one must take into consideration that nothing like it had ever happened before in the UK. Ten men stood in the dock; among them Reggie, Ronnie and Charlie Kray. Also Freddie Foreman. Regardless of who the other accused were, to put these four men on trial was a major achievement for Nipper Read and his team.

Freddie Foreman was an associate of the Krays from South

London. His criminal activity was more covert than that of the Krays. He had a good mind and assisted the Twins from time to time. He was in the dock as an accessory to the murder of Jack McVitie. Once the Kray trial was over Foreman and Reggie Kray stood trial for the murder of Frank Mitchell, for which they were both acquitted. Yet what the Mitchell trial did do was highlight that there were other murders for which the Twins may have been responsible.

CHAPTER 2
THE MITCHELL TRIAL

'Terror is the only weapon to wield against these people. To talk
kindly to them is only to encourage them. Demand nothing that
is not just, and never recede, and settle the whole in half an hour.'
LORD NELSON

It is important to explain how the Kray Firm fell to pieces
and how Nipper Read compiled his evidence against the
Twins in the unsuccessful Frank Mitchell trial, because the
two are inextricably linked.

The Twins masterminded Mitchell's escape from
Broadmoor and hid him in a London flat. The idea behind
this was to try and persuade the authorities to give Mitchell a
release date from prison. Teddy Smith wrote letters on
Mitchell's behalf to the authorities and national newspapers,
but the system wouldn't relent and the Twins were left with a
troublesome giant on their hands that they couldn't contain.
The only thing they could do in the end was persuade

Mitchell to get in a van on the pretence of spending Christmas in the countryside with Ronnie Kray, the reality being that they wanted to kill him. Sadly, they pulled it off.

A murder charge is easier to get when you have a body on the slab. However, Nipper Read didn't have a body for the McVitie or Mitchell murders, so how did he get his evidence for the murder of Frank Mitchell and take the case to trial?

The simple answer is through excellent police work.

One of the keys was Billy Exley. He was a member of the Kray Firm until he fell foul of the Twins and was threatened by them. Ronnie and Reggie told Exley that they would shoot not just him but his wife and children. Billy went into hiding and agreed to meet with Nipper Read, which he did on 14 May 1968. According to Read the meeting took place in Lambeth Palace Road. Exley was accompanied by Limehouse Willy and they were both in a very nervous state.

Billy admitted to Read that he looked after Frank Mitchell following his escape from Broadmoor. Read immediately gave him the customary police caution. He then asked him if he wanted to make a statement. Exley did. Two days later Exley arrived at Read's HQ in Tintagel House, on the southern Embankment of the Thames, where he gave a sworn statement that was signed by his solicitor, Tommy Edwards.

Read explained how scared Billy was in his book, *The Man Who Nicked The Krays*: 'He was still terrified someone would find out what he had done. "No one must know about it," he said to Edwards, "even in your office." Edwards assured him that the only two people who would know about it were he and his secretary.' This clearly shows the fear the Krays inspired. This was a man scared out of his wits by the glitzy

34

Kray brothers. He knew that they were after him and it was only in desperation that he agreed to talk to the police in return for protection.

Billy's statement was a good one. He explained, for example, that Mitchell had been brought to London, something that Read wasn't aware of. He then went on to explain how he hired the car that transported Mitchell. He then gave the name and address of the hire-car company. This was all important information, new pieces of the puzzle. But he went on to say even more, thus opening out the investigation. He explained that a hostess named Lisa had been brought in to live with Mitchell. Billy had gone to her flat, somewhere near the Bayswater Road, to pick up some clothes and drop her off at Frank's hideaway flat. According to Connie Whitehead (during a contemporary interview), who looked after Mitchell while staying at the flat, Frank and Lisa spent most of their time together in bed having sex.

Billy Exley made a second statement later in May, filling in more details concerning Mitchell and Lisa. This led Frank Cater – Read's number two – to make some investigations. He took Billy on a trip around West London to see if he could point out the flat where he had picked up the clothes. He did, so Cater went back and spoke to the occupier, who gave him Lisa's doctor's name and a photograph of her.

Cater then did a tour of the local hospitals and found a doctor who had treated Lisa in the past. He was given a family address in Leeds. Further enquiries were made through Lisa's mum, who gave an address in Battersea but explained that Lisa was about to embark on a world tour with her Australian boyfriend. Cater went to the address but found Lisa had gone.

It seemed as though Cater's luck had run out – she had left the week before. However, neighbours explained that the camper van that Lisa and her boyfriend had taken had broken down and they told Cater that they were still in the country. What's more, they knew the address of the garage where the camper was being repaired.

Cater followed the lead and spoke to the owner of the garage. The garage owner gave Cater the details of a car that he had hired out to the couple while the van was being repaired. He also explained that he believed that they were staying in Earl's Court. At 2:00 a.m. Cater found the hire-car parked outside a West London hotel. He had found Lisa and told her that she was to be taken to New Scotland Yard to talk about Frank Mitchell.

Cater later called Read and in the course of their conversation told him that he was bringing Lisa directly to Tintagel House instead of Scotland Yard. Lisa was escorted to a car and taken off for questioning. However, when the car she was in turned onto Lambeth Bridge – and thus away from the direction of Scotland Yard, where she thought that she was being taken – Lisa panicked. She suddenly thought that she was being kidnapped by the Kray Firm and was about to be bumped off. Again, here is another clear example of the fear the Twins were capable of instilling in their victims. Read explains: 'She'd realised that she was going over Lambeth Bridge and that was away from Scotland Yard, so as the car slowed down for the traffic, she jumped out and tried to jump over the bridge. She said, "I thought the Krays had come to get me," and that's the kind of terror the Krays generated. It was absolutely incredible. People would run a mile and jump off bridges. People believed in the all-seeing Kray eyes and were consequently very reluctant to make a statement or even talk to me.'

In fact, the Mitchell case was opened through similar extreme circumstances, as Read explained: 'A man went into a police station in West Ham and said that he wanted to see me, but before I got there he had had a change of heart and tried to commit suicide. He took pills and we had to get his stomach pumped. But, eventually, what he told us was that he was the owner of the flat where Mitchell lodged, so that became the start of the Mitchell enquiry. After that breakthrough we started our first murder investigation and charged all three of the Kray brothers and Albert Donoghue, Freddie Foreman and others with that first murder.'

So, the Mitchell murder was actually the first to be initiated by Read and his team, even though it would be the second case that would go to trial, after the Cornell and McVitie murder trial. But despite the evidence that Read and his team built up – and notwithstanding the string of suicide attempts by witnesses – the Mitchell trial was unsuccessful. Read explained why:

There are a series of reasons. The evidence was overwhelming in my view, but by the time that came to court, the Krays and their entourage had been charged with the murders of Cornell and McVitie and been sentenced to 30 years. So they came into court with those sentences and I think people thought that they had enough punishment. Albert Donoghue was my main witness who had actually been present when Mitchell was shot. Now I had charged him with the murder and I had to rescind the charge because he became the main prosecution witness. And the defence (for Reggie, Ronnie and Foreman) said that Donoghue was the real murderer and that the police got it right in the first place. So they said that the murder had nothing to do with them. This caused doubt that they exercised and put in the jurors' minds, coupled with the fact that there was little else they could get for punishment.

For clarity's sake, the people who were grouped together by Read and his team and put on trial for the Mitchell escape were: Reggie, Ronnie and Charlie Kray, Tommy Cowley, Wally Garelick, Conny Whitehead, John Dickson, Pat Connolly and Albert Donoghue [20].

Three members of the Firm turned against the Krays to give evidence at the Mitchell trial: Billy Exley, Albert Donoghue and Scotch Jack Dickson (the latter two assisted with the Mitchell escape). These were not fringe members of the Firm. For a long time they were trusted men. Then there was the hostess Lisa, who heard the gun shots that killed Mitchell, and the man who owned the flat. These last two both tried to commit suicide as a consequence of their involvement in the trial.

Lisa and the flat owner's fear of the Krays was justified, especially when you consider that the Twins tried to cover their tracks by killing the too-talkative Teddy Smith. Many people believe that Smith was killed to keep him quiet as he knew too much about the Mitchell murder. We will return to Smith's death in a later chapter.

The important thing to appreciate in all of this is that the Krays *were* responsible for Frank Mitchell's death. They helped him to escape from Dartmoor, they hid him and they were responsible for his murder when they didn't know what else to do with him. In this way we can say that although the Twins were only ever convicted of two murders, this one can also be held against them.

No great revelation perhaps, especially as it has been well documented on screen and in books in the past. The point is that this was just the tip of the iceberg. According to Nipper Read: 'There were other people too, there were a hell of a lot of other murders. I investigated seven murders myself. It was only the fact that we couldn't get enough evidence. It was like the Mitchell case, it was very difficult to charge them. We had no body and they weren't admitting to anything, and at the Old Bailey it was difficult to get anybody to give evidence.'

Read and his team tried hard to convict the Krays and their entourage for the Mitchell murder, as Freddie Foreman explained in his book *Respect*: 'I was arrested together with the Krays as an accessory to the murder of Jack "the Hat" McVitie and sent for trial at the Old Bailey on 28 February 1969. In April the same year, after I had been convicted of being an accessory after the fact of murder and sentenced to ten years, I faced a second murder rap, this time over Frank "The Mad Axeman" Mitchell (I was acquitted of this charge in 1975).'

So, the Mitchell trial went on a little longer than some people think. This goes to show how difficult it was to get a murder conviction. Read did well to get evidence enough for two murders and get the three Krays and their associates sent away for as long as he eventually did.

CHAPTER 3

WHY ONLY THREE MURDERS?

'Give me 40 divisions. Give me a force so strong as to fear
nothing and I will drive through to the heart.'
FIELD MARSHAL B L MONTGOMERY

As I've already explained, the Krays were only ever tried for
three murders. The main reasons for this were:

• So that Nipper Read could focus on the cases for which he
had the most compelling evidence in order to guarantee
a conviction.

• Because many of the people in the East End who knew
about the other murders were known to the Krays and their
associates – and knew the Krays themselves. So it was very
difficult to get people to go on the record against the Twins,
either because they were scared of Ronnie and Reggie, or
because they liked and respected them.

It is worth dwelling on this last point for a moment. When it comes to the suicide of Frances Shea, for example, many people fell into the trap of thinking that Reggie was so in love with her that when she died he fell into a deep depression and hit the bottle and went on the tranquillisers. The knock-on effect of this, they reasoned, was that Reggie could have pleaded Diminished Responsibility at the Jack McVitie trial. People were prepared to believe, in effect, that Reggie was not completely responsible for his actions, and should even be sympathised with. Well, to get Diminished Responsibility, you first have to plead guilty and Reggie Kray was not prepared to do that.

Well, that's not the truth I'm afraid. You can only rationalise the Krays' activities so much. To know the real truth about the Krays you had to have been there, to have known them and understood their personalities. This is why I devote a whole chapter to Frances' death in this book, as it cuts through some of the myths about the Krays and shows them for what they were. The truth about Frances' death needs to be told.

And this is not just my point of view. After Frances' death her parents tried to get her marriage to Reggie annulled. The reason was that Reggie never made love to Frances. She was just a bracelet that Reggie Kray could wear to his celebrity parties and show that she was his beautiful wife. The marriage was in fact never consummated and that is why Frances' parents didn't want her body to be dressed in her wedding dress in her coffin on the day of her funeral.

But there is even more to the death of Frances Shea than that. The poor girl was terrorised by the Krays and she was forced to marry Reggie due to a set of circumstances that will be discussed in Chapter 8.

The bottom line is that Frances committed suicide because of the Krays. No one really knows how many other people were driven to similar lengths. Consider the people who owned their own businesses, or were managers of businesses, who were squeezed like lemons for protection money. How many of them were driven to stress, illness, disease or even death through their traumatic association with the Twins? Then there was the everyday violence that the Firm meted out – the beatings and people being cut and chain-whipped on the floor. So many people were left at death's door, wrapped in blankets and dumped on the steps of the London Hospital. Who cares for these people? More importantly, what happened to them? Just because they didn't die the violence that they suffered gets overlooked, yet it undoubtedly affected them and their families. You don't get over being half-beaten to death; the scars are with you for the rest of your life. Imagine being branded with red–hot pokers, having your hair burned off with the searing heat inches away from your eyes and affecting your vision for the rest of your life.

There are mental scars to torture as well; you don't forget it, you carry it with you forever.

Yet ultimately, it is murder that we are concerned with here. Seven or 17 murders: in some respects the number is immaterial, so long as we accept that the Krays killed more than the two men that they were sentenced for. Some of the old East Enders know this and have assisted me in presenting names and stories to back this claim up. It is important that people don't create excuses for the Kray murders; after several murders surely the excuses begin to run out – not to mention the fact that murder is inexcusable anyway. Add to that the branding, cutting, chaining and beating of people and you begin to get an idea of what the Krays were really like. I want people to see the Krays for the monstrous villains they were and finally knock down their hero status. I can't deny that the occasional financial handout assisted some people, but where did the Krays get the money from in the first place? And even if they did help out some people, was it as many people as they hurt and terrified?

I think not.

It is a shame, to say the least, that the Krays were not brought to account for their other crimes. So what if it would have cost the tax payer more money. At least the truth about the Krays would be out there in the open at last.

But perhaps that is another reason why no other murders have been accounted for. Maybe society could only take so much horror when it came to the Krays. Once the truth regarding just some of their dealings became known then society said enough was enough and locked them up and threw away the key.

The Krays took a heavy punishment for the two murders for which they were convicted. Even the Twins themselves believed that it would have been better if they had been hanged. Perhaps society handed out to the Krays a little bit of retributive torture in that respect. Reggie Kray mentions in *Our Story* that when he was locked in his cell the night he began his 30-year sentence he broke down and cried. Remorse or self-pity? Either way, at least this shows that he knew what it felt like to be punished.

Although this book is mainly about the Kray murders I do want to go back to the beatings, cuttings, chain-whippings and overall reign of terror enjoyed by the Krays. Even if there had been no murders they were still hardened criminals who indulged in thuggish behaviour and who deserved to be punished.

Albert Donoghue has said in a TV documentary that it was one of his jobs on the Firm to wrap people injured by the Krays in blankets and place them on the doorstep of the London Hospital. Johnny Squibb, a man I didn't like at all, has added that many of those people left at the hospital were in a serious condition and could have died if they had not been treated.

To the Twins, all this chaining and slashing was good fun. It was a way of exerting their authority. To begin with they were the up-and-coming wide boys, hoping to catch the knowing eye of people like Jack Spot. They got noticed all right, taking a couple of GBH charges along the way. It was these lesser crimes on which the Krays' reputations were built. The celebrity image came later. And the legend of their criminal empire grew up even later than that. In fact, the Kray Firm was not any better or more successful than anybody else's Firm at the time. In its early days the Firm was even quite unprofessional and its members were known for squandering the riches they made. This was mainly down to Ronnie's disregard for money. It meant nothing to him.

When Reggie and Charlie opened the Double R club Ronnie was then on a stretch in prison. While Ronnie was not around his brothers became quite successful. Then Ronnie was released and decided to put his hand in the till anytime he felt like it. The truth is that the Krays weren't that astute with money. A few of the big names from the criminal world in the 1960s went off to the sunshine. But when it came to the Twins, they found that they didn't have enough money to follow suit. Unable to leave the country, they became caught in Nipper Read's net and, ultimately, wound up in prison while other villains enjoyed a life of freedom abroad. They didn't kid anyone in the end. Most people in the East End knew the real Krays and what they were about. Even today, more than 35 years after they were locked up, most people would say that they were wicked bastards and deserved everything they got.

CHAPTER 4

GEORGE CORNELL

'Already the sense of power was building in him as he held the Gun, weighing it in his hand, letting the light slide along the chased-silver barrel.'
LOGAN'S RUN, BY WILLIAM F NOLAN AND
GEORGE CLAYTON JOHNSON

Before we look at the other murders committed by the Krays, it is important to understand their more well-known homicides, not least because they reveal a pattern of behaviour that the Twins would continue to demonstrate. For example, Frances Shea committed suicide; so did other people. There is a reason for this: the Krays drove them to it. Also, it is a well-known fact in certain circles that Teddy Smith was killed by the Krays. Why? To discover the answer to that you need to understand the details of the Frank Mitchell killing, too.

But this is not the only reason to look again at the murders of Cornell, McVitie and Mitchell. It is also important to put the record straight. So many lies have been said in the past, so many half-truths, that it is imperative for the sake of the people who were murdered and their families to present the full details of their killings. This in itself takes more of the glamour away from the Twins. Look at the Cornell killing, for example. Legend has it that Ronnie Kray strode confidently into the Blind Beggar pub, calmly raised a Luger and pulled the trigger once to shoot George Cornell in the head and watched him fall *forwards* onto the bar. The truth of the killing, though, is a lot different and happened in a much more schizophrenic way, as you will see...

George Cornell was born in Stepney in the East End. I knew him in those days. In fact, I used to work in old Billingsgate Fish Market, where George owned a warehouse, and I used to help him out from time to time. Knowing him at first-hand, I can say that George was a very tough man who could handle himself against anyone, but he was not a liberty taker. In later years George married a lovely lady by the name of Olive, who came from South London, where George went to live. It was this South London connection that led to George joining the Richardson Gang.

So many lies have been told as to why Ronnie Kray shot George in the Blind Beggar pub, it is important to now know the truth of what is one of the most famous gangland killings in England. The story goes back a while before the night of the actual killing. George Cornell was drinking one evening in The Brown Bear pub in Dock Street, Stepney. Word got back to Ronnie Kray that George, a member of a rival gang, was in there so Ronnie decided to go over to the pub to teach Cornell a lesson [21]. When he got there Ronnie sent his driver in to the pub to check that Cornell was there and to tell him that he was wanted outside. As George left the pub he was confronted by Ronnie Kray. But instead of handing out any punishment to Cornell, Ronnie came unstuck that night because George Cornell ended up knocking him out. From that day on Cornell became an embarrassment to Ronnie.

Cornell was known to usually take a drink with the governor of The Blind Beggar on a Friday night, but it was a Wednesday night when he met his death in that pub. As bad luck would have it, he had dropped into the pub after visiting his friend Jimmy Andrews in the London Hospital close by.

The date was 9 March 1966. Ronnie Kray was drinking in the Lion pub in Tapp Street, just over half a mile away. He was with other members of the Firm, many of whom were in a good mood following the news that their rival Richardson gang had been involved in a brutal fight the night before in a Catford nightclub called Mr Smiths. Shots had been fired and one man had died. Eddie Richardson and Frankie Fraser, who were both injured in the shooting and who both ended up in hospital, had been charged by the police.

However, Ronnie Kray wasn't happy. He knew that Charlie Richardson was still in action, as he was away in South Africa on business at the time of the fight. He was even more unhappy that the murdered man was Richard 'Dickie' Hart, a friend of the Firm. When the phone rang in the Lion pub at 8:15 p.m. the person on the other end delivered the news that George Cornell was sitting in a pub close by. Given what had happened in Catford the previous evening, Ronnie Kray had an excuse for killing George Cornell – but this was not his real reason for murdering the man. It was his previous humiliation at the hands of George Cornell which ensured that Ronnie Kray would kill George Cornell when the right opportunity presented itself.

Ronnie told 'Scotch' Jack Dickson to get a car and drive him to the Blind Beggar. In the meantime he turned to his right-hand man, Ian Barrie, and told him to accompany him. All three strode out of the Lion. Other Firm members in the pub didn't know what was going on until Reggie told them: 'Cornell's round the Beggar's, and Ronnie's going round there. I hope he doesn't do anything stupid.'

In his book, *Born Fighter*, Reggie Kray stated that Ronnie had written up a dead pool list of people he wanted to knock off. One of them was Cornell. The phone call that came through to the Lion pub was the tip-off Ronnie wanted to strike somebody off his list. This is backed up by Laurie O'Leary, who wrote in his book, *Ronnie Kray – A Man Amongst Men*, that he visited Ronnie Kray the morning after the Catford shoot-out and Ronnie told him: 'That bastard Cornell wasn't there, Lol.' Laurie then went on to say that he could tell that Ronnie was 'hell-bent on some form of action against his enemy'. Having known Laurie O'Leary myself and being struck by his perception and knowledge of his old friend, it does seem painfully obvious that Ronnie had already made up his mind to do something about his nemesis.

So 'Scotch' Jack Dickson drove Ronnie and Ian Barrie to the Blind Beggar pub. Ronnie told Dickson to wait in the car while he and Barrie went inside the pub. They were both armed, but there does seem to be some confusion over the

LENNY HAMILTON WITH CRAIG CABELL

gun used by Ronnie. In *Nipper Read – The Man Who Nicked The Krays*, Read stated that the gun used was a Luger. However, the gun many people believe was used in the shooting is the one now in Scotland Yard's Black Museum and it is a 9mm Mauser – and this is the gun that Ronnie admits to having used in *My Story*. But in the first edition of his book *Me And My Brothers*, Charlie Kray says that he was puzzled that Ronnie should use a '9mm Luger'. He went on to say that it was a 'tricky weapon to use' and that Ronnie was no marksman and had less than perfect eyesight. Perhaps Charlie mistook the 9mm Mauser for a 9mm Luger. It's difficult to know who is right and who is wrong, but a possible solution to the dilemma is that Charlie and Ronnie came from a generation of shooters who would often generically call all 9mm automatics '9mm Lugers', whether they were actually Lugers or not.

The mystery is deepened by Albert Donoghue who, in his book *The Enforcer*, tells us about the disposal of the 'guns' used by Ronnie that night. He stated: 'Then I saw Ronnie give him two guns – a Luger, which looked new, and a small black automatic.' This raises a new question: Did Ronnie have two guns with him?

When Ronnie and Ian Barrie walked into the pub there were only five people in the bar: Albie Woods and Johnny Dale, who were having a quiet drink with George Cornell, and an old man who was sitting at the other end of the bar reading his newspaper. The final person was the barmaid, who was playing the Walker Brothers' 'The Sun Ain't Gonna Shine Anymore' on the pub record player (contrary to many accounts, the pub had no jukebox).

Cornell was drinking a light ale. Ronnie walked up to him. Cornell said, 'Well look who's here...' and Ronnie took out a gun and shot Cornell in the head. If this sounds pretty straightforward, the truth is anything but. If Ronnie Kray had held the gun close to Cornell's head, shooting him at close range, he wouldn't have fallen forward on to the bar as Ronnie Kray claimed in the Twins' joint autobiography, *Our Story*, where he wrote: 'He fell forward on to the bar. There was some blood on the counter. That's all that happened. Nothing more. Despite any other account you may have read of this incident, that was what happened.' Not quite, though, because a shot fired so close would mean that the momentum of the blast would most definitely have blown Cornell off his stool. Matters have not been helped by the fact that Ronnie Kray later changed his account for *My Story*, in which he stated that Cornell 'fell off his stool'.

Cornell's friends had vanished into the toilet as soon as Ronnie approached and the barmaid simply went hysterical. In order to tell the truth of what happened that night it is important to look at the records and photographs in the National Archive. In fact, the barmaid's statement is quite helpful, too. She claimed that she didn't see Ronnie Kray enter the pub. She only knew that he was in the bar when he walked past her on his way to the bottom of the saloon where Cornell sat between his two friends. This statement discredits the previously believed story that Barrie shot both barrels of a shotgun into the ceiling on entering the pub.

'Mrs X' (as the barmaid was called at the trial) recalled that Ronnie Kray was wearing a dark blue suit, a tie and no glasses (he was wearing glasses at the trial). He was still walking towards the bottom of the bar when Cornell said, 'Well look who's here...'

Now, here's the interesting bit. The version of the story that seems to fit the public's perception is this: Ronnie came to a halt beside the fourth stool down the bar, a 45-degree angle and about five to six feet (2m) away from Cornell. He raised his gun and fired. The bullet ripped a hole straight through Cornell's forehead, just above his right eyebrow, exiting through the back of the head and passing into the bar behind him and burying itself in a wall.

If this is the case, then several things do not quite ring true. For this account to be accurate it would mean that after the bullet passed through Cornell's head it would have travelled roughly in a straight line under an arch and into the back bar. However, it is unusual for a bullet to follow a straight line after passing through somebody's head (even though a diagram in the National Archive claims that this is what happened). It is also clear that Cornell was blown off his stool by the blast, his blood and tissue pumping out onto the floor of the bar. After being shot Cornell turned slightly to his right – in Ronnie's direction – blood now flowing from his mouth. Because of the angle of his body on the floor, he was not asphyxiating. He then lost consciousness. The record player behind the bar got stuck, adding to the chaos that ensued.

As it is unusual for a 9mm bullet to pass through somebody's head, under an arch and into a wall in a straight line, how is it that a bullet did in fact end up lodged in the wall? Was it the case that this bullet was the result of a second shot being fired? A shot that missed Cornell entirely and went straight into the wall, passing by the already mortally wounded Cornell as he fell to the floor. The barmaid's court statement said: 'I can remember the shot that hit Cornell and another one distinctly but after that it was just a lot of noise. There was possibly another shot, but it was so noisy that I was confused. The shot which hit Cornell was the first shot I heard. I am certain of that.'

It does indeed seem clear from this that Ronnie fired two shots that night. Checking the reports in the National Archive we find a total of three bullets found at the scene of the crime. The 9mm was the one that hit Cornell, but the other two bullets were .32-calibre and were found in a chair leg and on the floor (having passed through a bar stool). The presence of these .32-calibre bullets clearly suggests the presence of a second hand gun.

All of this substantiates Albert Donoghue's comment that Ronnie handed over two hand guns for disposal later. If we want to take this a step further, we can rationalise the killing by recognising that between 1900 and 1904, the Luger pistol was made in .32 calibre. Is this why people have confused the Luger and the Mauser in the Cornell murder? Ronnie was carrying both guns.

When the barmaid stated in court that she heard 'the shot that hit Cornell and another one distinctly', we know her statement is accurate. When she then states, 'There was possibly another shot, but it was so noisy that I was confused', we know that she has a very good memory of events, simply because there *was* a third shot. Ronnie Kray fired three times, only hitting Cornell once.

Ian Barrie stated that Ronnie hit Cornell twice. We know this is wrong when we read the post-mortem examination in the National Archive. But if Ronnie shot two rounds from the second gun – the Luger – after the single shot from the Mauser, and if he shot them quickly, then three shots would sound like two. .

That's two eye-witness reports coming together. Furthermore, as Barrie had a shotgun and two hand guns were later disposed of – as witnessed by Albert Donoghue – we have a great deal of evidence to suggest that three shots were fired. It is also important to recognise that the final two shots clearly missed, but one went through the top of a bar stool and was found on the floor. Was that the barstool next to Cornell or his own spinning in the air? We also know that the other bullet hit a chair leg, possibly as Ronnie lurched forward after responding to Cornell's fall.

The picture that now emerges is of a more urgent Ronnie Kray, not the cool customer that he was keen to portray himself as [22]. According to 'Scotch' Jack Dickson, when Ronnie got back in the car he was genuinely excited. 'I actually shot him,' Ronnie said. He was pleased – excited – by his work. After the shooting Ronnie, Barrie and Dickson went back to the Lion and Ronnie told Reggie what he had done. Reggie allegedly wasn't impressed; he was probably worried about the number of witnesses in the pub.

Everybody was ordered to leave the Lion, driving cars in different directions in case the police were watching them. One man, known at the trial as Mr D, had the following conversation with Reggie on leaving the Lion [23]:

'Where are we going?'

'Just drive off the manor,' Reggie said.

'Where do I drive to?'

'Head towards Walthamstow.'

'What's happening?'

'Ronnie's just shot Cornell. Get off the manor. Head towards Walthamstow. Drive carefully. I don't want to get a pull. Take your time.'

This conversation is important to quote because it gives credence to the fact that Reggie Kray was cold and dangerous. His brother had just killed a man, but he calmly deals with the situation. He's not running around screaming and shouting. He's not arguing with Mr D either, despite what could be construed as aggravating questions. You suddenly understand a little more about Reggie Kray.

Ronnie ended up in the Stowe Club in Hoe Street, Walthamstow. He changed his clothes, having the set he wore to the murder burnt, then arranged for cat burglar Charlie Clark to dispose of the guns, which he duly did. The Mauser was recovered from the mud of the River Lea in 1993 and placed in the Black Museum; the Luger is still missing, possibly dumped elsewhere.

Reggie had organised Firm members to go out and find the witnesses who had been in the Blind Beggar that night. Their job was to bully them into silence. This was successfully carried out and even the barmaid failed to identify Ronnie Kray in an identity parade soon afterwards. Such was the fear the Krays instilled in their victims. Remember, just two years later people were contemplating suicide rather than give evidence against them for the pending trial, believing that the

Krays' eyes were everywhere, watching every move and, if anybody did anything wrong, they would, in Reggie's words, 'disappear off the face of the earth'.

We'll return to those words – one of Reggie's favourite phrases – later on.

Coming back to George Cornell, let's look closely at the unglamorous truth of his demise. The first thing to know is that Cornell didn't die instantly, but lay bleeding on the floor of the pub. It was the manager of the Blind Beggar, Patsy Quill, who called the ambulance and then tried to make George comfortable until help arrived. It wasn't long before the dying man was taken a couple of hundred yards to the London Hospital – the same hospital that he had been in hours earlier when visiting a friend. Jaivant Chhotey Lal [24] examined Cornell at the hospital on his admission at 8:49 p.m. He stated that the victim had a 'penetrating wound in the forehead and a wound at the back of his head almost in the middle of the occiput... [he was] transferred to Maida Vale Hospital' [25]. Raymond Leonard George Newcombe was the house surgeon at Maida Vale Hospital. He made the following statement at the trial: 'At 9:30 p.m. that day a patient was admitted to my hospital... He was identified to me as George Cornell. I identified him as the man shown in photo 1 of *Ex.3*. He was unconscious on arrival and there was a wound on his forehead and at the back of his head. Those wounds were consistent with him having been shot in the head. He was given the appropriate treatment at that stage and taken to the operating theatre. He died, before any operative treatment could be commenced, at 10:29 p.m. His heart stopped at 10:29 p.m.'

George Cornell lived for approximately two hours after being shot by Ronnie Kray.

At Walthamstow, the Firm – headed by Ronnie – were huddled round the radio awaiting the news of Cornell's death. A report of the shooting came through at midnight. Shortly afterwards, it was announced that Cornell was dead. A cheer went up from the Firm. Perhaps they wouldn't have been so happy if they had known that precisely three years later Ronnie and Reggie would be just one day away from receiving 30-year prison sentences.

Ronnie had made a very public killing, which is why we are able to analyse it so well. However, the other Kray murders were not as public. In some cases there was not even a corpse. This absence of bodies would cause Nipper Read a lot of problems down the line. But having said that, let's not forget that when Cornell's wife Olive found out that he had been shot dead, she went round to Vallance Road and threw a brick through the window. It was obvious to Olive – and others – that Ronnie Kray had committed the murder. The same principle applies to other murders committed in the area – people in the East End usually knew who committed them, even if the police had difficulty proving it.

It is important at this juncture to add a story that has been previously – and incorrectly – linked to the Cornell murder: the assault by Frankie Fraser on Eric Mason, a friend of the Krays.

There is a school of thought that suggests that because Eric was badly slashed by Fraser – on behalf of the Richardsons – Ronnie took revenge on one of their men, Cornell. The truth is that nobody knows. However, let us look at what happened to Eric and how this misrepresentation came about.

Frankie Fraser came from Camberwell, south of the river. He was on the Richardson Firm and an enemy of the Kray twins. By his own admission, he has served 42 years of his life behind bars. Part of his time in prison was served after the Catford shoot-out at Mr Smiths. While he was still in prison Fraser met up with the Twins and offered to stand for them as a witness when their trial came up – knowing full well that they hated his guts and at one time wanted him dead!

Well known in the criminal world, Fraser later became something of a household name after writing his memoirs and appearing in several TV programmes about the underworld. In one such documentary about the Richardsons, called *Crime Story*, Fraser told the story of how he once threw Eric Mason out of a club and whisked him away in a car. However, he forgot to mention that in doing so he had had plenty of help. Fraser and his cohorts took Eric to a basement and set about hitting and cutting him to pieces until Fraser attempted to hit Eric on the head with an axe. Eric saw the weapon coming and blocked the blow with his hand, which left him with a very nasty scar. When Fraser was asked what he did with the axe he said that he left it embedded in Mason's head, 'A lovely axe,' he said. Fraser concluded the story by saying that he then put Eric in a car and dumped him outside a hospital with the axe still in his head.

Part of the reason for including Eric's story at the end of this chapter isn't because of its possible connection to the Cornell murder. It's here as an example of how a violent anecdote can be incorrectly related over time. Let's face it: the

Cornell murder has been incorrectly told and re-told ever since the Twins' joint autobiography, *Our Story*, was released in the late 1980s. That's more than 20 years, during which time the Kray movie starring Gary and Martin Kemp added a designer interpretation of the story, thus making the legend even more difficult to break down.

The story of Cornell's murder as told above is probably the most accurate you could wish to read. It's more unglamorous than other versions, but it is a *true* version. Importantly, it highlights the madness of Ronnie Kray.

Returning to the Eric Mason story, let's get the truth about Frankie Fraser's blood-lust directly from Eric Mason himself.

Back in February 2006, I helped to make a DVD for Eric in the garden of the Blind Beggar pub. With us that day, looking as beautiful as ever, was Flanagan, the first Page Three girl. I sat next to Eric Mason and his son, Jeff, and found them to be very nice people. As I got talking, I asked Eric about the axe that Fraser said he left in his head. It was then that Eric spread his hand on the table for me to see where the axe had hit his hand between his fingers. He also said that his body was covered in scars and that he had needed more than 300 stitches after the attack. Throughout all of this he never went to the police and for that I call him a real man. Fraser didn't leave the axe in Eric's head or for that matter drop him outside a hospital. He left him on waste ground.

You see how stories become distorted over time when people play Chinese whispers?

Some people will ask why bother getting into such detail and over-analysing everything? After all, the end result is the same: a person was killed and the Twins were eventually punished accordingly. While this is true, it is the fact that so much glamour has attached itself to the Krays that angers me and I feel that I have to break down their underserved reputation by giving a more accurate interpretation of events.

In this spirit, let's move on to the end of Jack 'the Hat' McVitie.

CHAPTER 5

JACK MCVITIE

'Jack said the room felt cold and musty at the same time; he had to get out.'
BLACK AND BLUE, BY IAN RANKIN

I knew Jack McVitie well but I wasn't there when he died. A good friend of mine knew something about what happened that night and he told me all about it. My friend was Ronnie Bender. He was a man everyone in the East End admired. He had never been in trouble with the police. He was an ex-army man; a soldier. It was in the army that Ronnie met his lovely wife, Buddy. Her father was in the army and stationed in the same camp as Ronnie Bender.

When Ronnie met Buddy it was love at first sight, and after a long courtship they got married. Ronnie had served out his time in the army and he and Buddy set up home on the Isle of Dogs, in the East End, where they still lived until quite recently with their three grown-up hard-working sons.

Ronnie had a very good-looking sister by the name of Doreen, who was well known and liked around the East End. Doreen was a very good friend of the Kray twins and they liked her for her honesty. Doreen would say what she thought and if you did not like what she said, that was just too bad.

Doreen married Teddy Farmer, a man that was to become a good friend of mine. I first met him while we were in the same prison. I am sad to say that both Teddy and Doreen have now passed away. As Doreen knew the Kray twins so well, Ronnie Kray once confided in her that he was looking for a driver that he could trust (Ronnie couldn't drive himself). Doreen told him that her brother Ronnie was looking for work and he was taken on. Ronnie Bender became the last driver Ronnie Kray would ever have, looking after him for his final nine months of freedom before the whole Kray Firm was nicked.

Ronnie Bender was a big, strong man. He wasn't violent and if he couldn't do you a good turn then he most certainly wouldn't do you a bad one. He was a good-looking lad and was more than capable of looking after himself. I'm relating all this because I do feel sorry for him. At the time that he was hired by the Krays they knew that it was only a matter of time before they were going to be nicked by Nipper Read and his team. You see, the Krays cared for nobody but themselves.

Ronnie Bender's world was turned upside down the night he was invited to a party at 'Blonde' Carol Skinner's house in Evering Road, Hackney. He knew that the Twins had the hump with Jack McVitie for slagging them off, but never in a million years did he suspect that the so-called party was all a front to get Jack there for Reggie to mutilate him. When the deed had been done the Twins, cowards that they were, fled the crime scene, leaving Ronnie Bender to get rid of the body and clear up the mess.

When the Kray case finally came up at the Old Bailey, Ronnie Bender was given a 20-year prison sentence for his part in getting rid of Jack's body; the two Lambrianou brothers – Chris and Tony – received 15 years each. These three men all stayed loyal to the Kray twins, keeping their mouths shut throughout and after the trial. But what loyalty did any one of them get from the Twins? Nothing. When the Twins were offered a deal by Nipper Read to hold their hands up to the murders of Cornell and McVitie in order to let the rest of the Firm go free, the Twins said no. If they were going to go down – as they knew they were – then they were prepared to take the rest of the Firm with them.

To his dying day you never heard Ronnie Bender complain about the punishment he took. After all was said and done, he was in the wrong place at the wrong time. In my heart I will always admire Ronnie for his loyalty. Ronnie Bender passed away while I was writing this book, after suffering two heart attacks. God bless you Ronnie, you will always be in my thoughts. Like Jack McVitie, the Twins took away a large part of your life and this chapter is as much to your memory and the man you were as it is to Jack and the person he was.

I believed what Ronnie Bender told me and this was confirmed when I later read Chris Lambrianou's book, *Escape From The Kray Madness*. On page 117 McVitie is quoted as saying to Chris that, 'I don't trust your brother'. They were standing at the bar with the Mills brothers just hours before McVitie was killed by Reggie Kray. Chris replied that Tony was as 'right as rain', but once again McVitie shook his head and said he wasn't convinced. Chris then writes: 'A few minutes later, Tony was standing beside me. "There's a party at Blonde Carol's," he said. "Plenty of birds and all the rest of it. Let's go there".' The party was only around the corner.

As things turned out, Jack proved to be a good judge of character.

In his book *Inside The Firm*, Tony Lambrianou stated that he was left with Jack's body. He wasn't. He had lost his bottle and had left after the murder, but was ordered back by the Krays to help Ronnie Bender tidy up. When Lambrianou got back to Blonde Carol's flat the only two people that were there were Ronnie Bender and Chris Lambrianou. Everyone else had gone. This is all contradictory to what Tony has said in his book and on screen. He's dead now but it's got to be said for the record: Tony Lambrianou was never on the Kray Firm because the Krays didn't trust him. Reggie Kray said Tony was just an errand boy, not a 'former Kray boss', as he has wrongly been described. Even Billy Exley didn't trust him. So, was Tony right and everybody else wrong? I don't think so.

Ronnie Bender told me that he was out drinking with Ronnie Hart and the Twins the night Jack McVitie was killed. Bender told me that both the Twins were getting drunk and decided to go to the Regency Club, but on the way there they first went to Blonde Carol's place. Bender said that Blonde Carol was home at the time and let them in. It was Ronnie Kray who told her that they wanted to use her place to have a party and that she should go across the road and stay with a friend. At first she was reluctant to do so because her two children were asleep upstairs. The Twins insisted and told her that she would be doing them a big favour. So Carol left the house.

Ronnie Bender and Ronnie Kray were left with Hart and the two young boys they had taken with them. Reggie said that he was popping round to the Regency Club to order some drinks. Hart was acquitted of any criminal involvement at the trial. At that precise time the two Lambrianou brothers were drinking in the downstairs bar with McVitie. The place was packed, as it always was on a Saturday night, and the Twins knew that Jack would go there. Reggie went to the office in the Regency and asked Tony Barry to go and fetch Tony Lambrianou, which he duly did. Reggie told Lambrianou to take McVitie to Blonde Carol's, promising a party with lots of birds and booze. Knowing how much Jack liked a party, they were sure that he would be up for it.

That was when Tony Barry was handed a gun by Reggie Kray, right in front of Tony Lambrianou. Reggie told Tony Barry that if he didn't take the gun to Blonde Carol's he would have no option but to shoot Jack in his own club. I must say that it was a very shrewd move by Reggie to try to implicate the Barry boy, who had no option but to agree to do the task [26]. Reggie soon went round to Blonde Carol's himself and placed Ronnie Hart at an upstairs window to let him know when Jack arrived. When the two Lambrianou and Mills brothers arrived at Blonde Carol's, Ronnie Hart came downstairs to let them in. Ronnie Bender told me that when Reggie Kray came back to Blonde Carol's he said that the booze was on its way. He said this to take away any suspicion as to the fate that awaited McVitie.

Ronnie Bender went on to say that the two young boys were dancing in the middle of the room to the music when McVitie walked in, expecting to see a party going on. Ronnie Kray told him that he had had enough of McVitie slagging them off and of going to the Regency with a gun to shoot him and Reggie. With that, Reggie pulled out a gun and put it to Jack's head and pulled the trigger twice, but the gun would not fire so Ronnie smashed a glass in Jack's face. Jack struggled free and in doing so he put his elbow through the window [27]. Ronnie Hart and Tony Lambrianou got hold of Jack, forcing his arms up his back, and Ronnie Kray was shouting: 'Go on Reg, kill the fucking bastard.'

Reggie was handed a large knife, which he stabbed into Jack's face. Ronnie Kray was still shouting: 'Go on Reg, give it to him up the guts.' Reggie did. Again and again, until Jack's lifeless body fell to the floor. To make sure that he was dead, Reggie slit Jack's throat.

While all this was going on, Connie Whitehead arrived and seeing Chris Lambrianou sitting on the stairs crying, asked him what was wrong. 'I didn't come here to see all this,' Chris said. Connie drove Chris home and told him to forget what had gone on. Connie Whitehead then went home himself. Once Chris was home he realised that Tony was still in Blonde Carol's house so he went back, carrying a gun, in order to find his brother. But when he got back to Carol's place the only person there was Ronnie Bender. 'Where is everybody?' Chris asked. Bender told him that everyone had gone. 'Run away including your Tony,' he said.

It was then that Bender told Chris that Jack was dead downstairs and that the Krays had left him there to get rid of

Jack's body and throw it onto the railway lines, which was quite a distance away. After he had done that Bender was to clean up the flat.

I do admire Chris Lambrianou, because he has always stated that he was never on the Kray Firm and I know that he did not like a lot of the things they were into and what they got up to. So good luck to him. He is well away from the East End now and enjoying his new life with his new family. As for his brother Tony, he brought about his own brother's downfall. Like Tony, Chris spent 15 years in prison. To tell you the truth, I did not like Tony Lambrianou because he thought too much of himself. He was never on the Kray Firm. He was a fringe member. As for Jack McVitie, he was more of a man than anyone on the Firm because he was not a yes man. Jack was his own man and I admired him because he said what he thought and nobody can blame him for the way he was. You speak as you find and I always liked Jack McVitie.

Jack McVitie's end was a very unpleasant affair. As Nipper Read wrote in his book, *Nipper Read, The Man Who Nicked The Krays*: 'So at last I knew the full grisly details of McVitie's death, which would turn most people's stomachs. Even so, apparently, Reggie would later admit [in *Our Story*]: "I did not regret it at the time and I don't regret it now. I have never felt a moment's remorse". '

I have told you about McVitie's murder as related to me by a dear friend of mine who was there. Ronnie Bender was a nice man and I have no reason to doubt his sobering version of the story. But, for Jack's memory, I want to relate a little of the build-up to his problems with the Krays. This will allow you to understand Jack McVitie a little more. So, let me now tell you about Jack and one of his colleagues.

This guy was a good boxer. He was liked by everyone in the East End and was very friendly with the Twins. In fact, he was more like one of the family. He was no gangster but was seen in their company quite frequently. That was until the Twins sent him and Jack McVitie to pick up a lorry load of stolen gear.

McVitie dropped the boxer off on the way back and then dropped some of the goods off for himself, knowing full well that the Twins would only pay him a pittance for his work. When the Twins found out that some of the goods were missing from the lorry, Reggie went straight around to the boxer's house and, in front of his wife, shot him in the foot. Reggie gave him no opportunity to account for himself. He had no idea what had happened to the missing goods. When Reggie found out he went to see Jack. Knowing Jack as I did, he must have talked his way out of a hiding when Reggie confronted him.

On another occasion somebody went round to the Krays and told them that a certain car dealer had been slagging them off. This was a car dealer who had been paying the Twins protection money and allowing them to use his cars when they needed them. Just like the boxer, they never gave the car dealer a chance to defend himself. Reggie shot him in the leg. By this time, shooting people had become a habit with the Twins, along with cutting people up. In fact, Ronnie enjoyed cutting people across the arse, because when it was stitched up a person couldn't sit down without breaking the stitches. I was told by a top police physician that Ronnie Kray was a raving lunatic who got sexual pleasure by seeing people in pain.

He used to come his lot and I can now see that there was a lot of truth in what the police physician said, because when Ronnie was burning me with red-hot pokers he was making all sorts of funny noises. He grunted and groaned as if he was having sex and reaching his final climax. With all the pain that Ronnie and Reggie dished out to people I will go so far to say that in my honest opinion they were both fucking mad. Just look at the way that Reggie murdered Jack McVitie. What sort of person acts like that? Jack McVitie was a very good friend of mine, and many stories that I cannot accept have come out about him in all of the Kray books. Tony Lambrianou was one of those people who wrote and said wrong things about Jack. He would never have said anything about Jack on television if Jack had still been alive.

I was on Nicky Campbell's television programme with Tony Lambrianou when he was asked why Reggie killed Jack. Tony's answer was that Jack challenged the Twins. In his book with Freddie Foreman, *Getting It Straight – Villians Talking*, Lambrianou said that if he had known that I was going to be on the programme he would have walked out, yet he failed to say that before the programme started when he was standing right beside me! Then, on the last television programme, *The Final Word*, which featured Reggie Kray, Lambrianou said that the Twins didn't know what they were doing the night Reggie killed Jack.

Johnny Barry and his brother Tony said on national television that Tony Lambrianou was the 'Judas' that night when Reggie killed Jack McVitie in cold blood. I have been in pubs around the East End where I have heard Tony Lambrianou boast about being on the Kray Firm. He loved all the attention. He was never a gangster; possibly a cardboard one.

The people I feel sorry for over the McVitie murder are Blonde Carol, because they abused her trust and used her flat at 65 Evering Road, Ronnie Bender for the 20 years he served in prison, and Chris Lambrianou for the 15 years he served. Then there is Connie Whitehead, who again was not involved but still served his time – almost a decade. None of these people were told what was going to happen that night. The only person who really knew that Reggie was going to kill McVitie was Tony Lambrianou. While he was drinking with his brother Chris and the Mills brothers in the Regency Club, which was just around the corner from Blonde Carol's place, he disappeared from their company for three quarters of an hour. He was in the Regency office when the gun was presented. And then he let his brother go to that so-called party knowing what was to happen to Jack.

Strangely, the reason why Jack went to the Regency Club that night was to shoot and kill the Twins – not with a shotgun, as Laurie O'Leary said in his book, but with a gun that I bought for him when I was at a party one night in the East End. It was an American service revolver. If the Twins had been there he would have killed them both and done us all a favour.

Jack had the needle with them. The reason why was that they had stuck up a gold bullion job worth £300,000. But when the job was done and the money paid out, all the Twins gave McVitie for his cut was £4,000. A pittance in comparison to what they made. They bought a large house in

Suffolk with the money. That was the real reason why Jack wanted to shoot them. They stitched him up.

Now you understand why Jack acted the way he did with the Twins. Jack McVitie was a good thief. He worked with a gang of safe blowers. He wasn't a petty crook as some people have stated in the past. In fact, let me tell you another story about Jack McVitie: in the early 1960s I had a meet with Jack in a pub in Bow called Kitson's. We were doing some business at the time. I was standing at the bar when Jack walked in. We had a few drinks together and once we had concluded our business, Jack went to leave and in doing so he spotted some old ladies and gentlemen sitting round a table having their brown and milds or Guinness. Jack reached into his pocket and withdrew a bundle of money, putting it on their table and saying: 'Here, that will keep you all in drinks for a while.' That was the type of man Jack McVitie was. I know at times when he had too much to drink he could be a right menace, but that didn't make him a bad person. I have seen people do much worse than Jack when they've had a drink.

I have seen with my own eyes how some villains have cowed down to the Twins, so I have the utmost respect for George Cornell and Jack McVitie because they were not afraid of the Krays. The Twins knew that too. This is why they took a back-up of Firm members with them when they went to kill Cornell and McVitie.

It is true that McVitie kept the down payment that the Twins gave him to kill Leslie Payne. As far as Jack was concerned, it was a bit back for what they owed him on the bullion job. Nevertheless, Jack and Billy Exley did go to Leslie Payne's house to kill him. Jack was tasked with this because the Krays had allegedly been informed by a contact at Scotland Yard that Payne had informed on them. When Mrs Payne opened the door to McVitie and Exley she said that her husband wasn't home, so they got back in their car and drove off. Leslie Payne didn't know how close to death he came that day. You see, the Krays would put Firm members up to make killings for them which the Firm boys didn't really want to do. If McVitie and Exley were heavy-weight killers they would have searched Payne out, but that never happened.

I hope this further perception allows you to understand a little more about Jack McVitie and the man he was – and the men that the Twins were. McVitie wasn't a bad man, but now he is just a murder victim whose death is somehow more important than his life and that is unfair. I hope I have now restored some of the man's integrity in these pages.

But what happened to McVitie's body? It was never recovered, which meant that his family couldn't have a proper funeral for him. Ask Freddie Foreman and he'll tell you that he had a contact with a deep-sea trawler and that McVitie, along with another Kray victim, Frank Mitchell, was weighed down inside chicken wire and given a burial at sea. However, the Krays did have other ways to dispose of the bodies of their victims. Before we look at that let us first learn how the Lambrianous and Ronnie Bender actually disposed of Jack McVitie's body, separating the fact from the fiction.

To begin with, McVitie's car was driven round to the front of the house. Then came the difficult bit: getting McVitie's body into the car without being seen. The street was intermittently busy, and there were a few abortive attempts before the coast was clear and they could get the body into the car. They couldn't put it into the boot because it was full of junk – it would have been difficult anyway in an Austin Mini! – so they had to put it on the floor between the front and back seats.

It was decided that Tony Lambrianou would drive McVitie's car and dispose of the body somewhere south of the river, well away from the area they were in. Chris Lambrianou and Ronnie Bender followed in another car. Both men were armed. If for any reason Tony was stopped by the police, they could possibly cause a disturbance and get Tony to safety.

It was past 1:00 a.m. when Tony drove down Evering Road to Clapton, along Mare Street into Cambridge Heath Road, Commercial Road and then into the Rotherhithe Tunnel. It was then that Tony saw a police car coming towards him. This shouldn't have presented a problem, but McVitie's car was a wreck and would have attracted the police's attention. Apparently, the car had only one functioning headlight so Tony put his foot down to get out of there; consequently, Ronnie and Chris lost him for a little while.

By about 2:00 a.m., Ronnie and Chris were still driving around looking for Tony. Finally they found him, picked him up and drove back to the East End. Tony told them that he had lost the police and left the car beside a church. He had simply locked it up and legged it, throwing the car keys into the Regent Canal.

The Lambrianou brothers dropped Ronnie Bender off at Hackney Road and went home. Bender then went to Harry Hopwood's flat, around the corner from the Hackney Road.

The Twins were there with Ronnie Hart. It was there that Reggie's hand was treated as he had received a cut during the McVitie murder [28].

Bender told them that the body had been dumped in South London. Ronnie Kray went berserk, believing that leaving the body there would implicate Freddie Foreman in McVitie's murder. Bender was sent round to Charlie Kray's. Charlie was still enjoying a night out but Bender told Charlie's wife Dolly what had happened. When Charlie came home, he went over to Hopwood's flat and had an argument with the Twins. Charlie told them that they were stupid killing somebody at a 'party' in front of witnesses. He then told them that he was finished with them and went home to bed. The story then goes that someone was sent over to Freddie Foreman's place. It was now 3:00 a.m. Foreman was told what had happened, but all he wanted to do was go back to bed.

Before dawn broke, around 6:00 a.m., Freddie Foreman got up and drove over to the Rotherhithe Tunnel area to find McVitie's car. Alfie Gerrard followed Foreman as a back-up, but there were a lot of churches around the area so it took them a little while to find the right one. Foreman looked in the back window of a parked car and was thankful that it was a wet morning, as it was perfectly obvious that there was a body lying in the back. People were walking past the car, with their heads down because of the rain, so were not inquisitive enough to look into the windows of a parked vehicle.

Foreman broke into the car and drove it away. Not only was one headlight not working but the windscreen wipers were also broken. Foreman was not a happy man. He knew he was taking too many chances. But he had given his word that he

Billy 'Jack' Frost. One of the most loyal and covert members of the Kray Firm.

Top: Friends reunited: Lenny Hamilton, Billy Frost and Eric Mason at the Blind Beggar, December 2005.

Right: This photograph was staged just so Jimmy Evans could be identified by a would-be assassin, from left to right: Tommy Cowley, Albert Donoghue, Reggie Kray, Joe Wilkins and Jimmy Evans.

Bottom right: At a Christine Keeler party, Reggie Kray (far right), Eric Mason (centre, looking off camera).

Top: George and Allan Dixon outside the first pub the Krays ever owned, the Carpenter's Arms, Cheshire Street. It was a couple of hundred yards from the Kray home at Vallance Road.

Bottom: Before the Krays, George and Allan Dixon (top second and first right) had their own Firm with (bottom left), Ronnie Bender; all three fine men.

OCTOBER 17, 1951   BOXING NEWS   5

No you're not seeing double, just identical twins. On your left: The Krays, Ron and Reg. On your right: The Smiths, Jackie and " Southpaw " Albert.

TWINS

Why not match the Krays and Smiths? *asks* '*Ringwise*'

Where Are They Now ? No. 98   *by Norman Brown*

Sharkey upset champions

IF any ambitious matchmaker is at a loss for a couple of attractive supporting contests may I suggest the Smiths v. the Krays. Never heard of them you may say. Quite rightly, neither match will make a lot of difference to British or even Area championships, but it offers probably a unique opportunity of matching a pair of identical twins.

Top: Reggie Kray sent Eric Mason this signed photo shortly after Ronnie's funeral. It reads: 'Eric and family, Ron and I together in spirit. Walk as one. God bless. Your friend, Reg Kray, 1996'.

Bottom: If the Twins had stayed at the boxing or even in the army, maybe, just maybe, their lives could have been different, as shown in this fascinating article pairing the Krays against identical twins from Elland in Yorkshire.

Top: Laurie O'Leary was a close friend of the Krays throughout their lives. Never a gangster, Laurie was a much loved and respected member of his community.

Bottom: When the *East London Advertiser* heard of this book and the people involved they made it headline news.

After the funeral:
Charlie Kray posed for
these previously unreleased
photographs shortly after
brother Ronnie's funeral,
Croydon, 1995.

Left: Eric Mason (far left), Freddie Foreman and Roy Shaw (third and fourth left).

Bottom: Reunited after 37 years, Leonard 'Nipper' Read and Lenny Hamilton.

Top: The best of friends –
Lenny Hamilton and
Billy Frost talking
about the nuances of
this book, Greenwich,
December 2005.

Right: Lenny Hamilton's
original court summons
to give evidence against
Ronnie Kray.

IN THE INNER LONDON AREA.

SOUTH WESTMINSTER
PETTY SESSIONAL DIVISION

TO:

Leonard HAMILTON

(1) YOU ARE HEREBY ORDERED,

Ronald to attend and give evidence at the trial of
KRAY

before the:

current sitting of the Central Criminal Court, Old Bailey, London, E.C.4.

or at such other Court as you may be directed.

Dated the *10th* day of *July* 19 *69*.

Metropolitan Stipendiary Magistrate
Justice of the Peace for the Inner London Area.
sitting at

Magistrates' Court.

or By order of the Court

BOW STREET

Clerk of the Magistrates' Court.

NOTE:
Under Section 3(1) of the Criminal Procedure (Attendance of Witnesses) Act 1965 a person who
disobeys a witness order without just excuse may be punished with imprisonment not exceeding three
months and a fine.

would deal with McVitie's body and, as Freddie Foreman maintains, he arranged for McVitie's body to be buried at sea. ☙ The truth is, the Krays leaned on other people to do a lot of their dirty work. Freddie Foreman assisted them from time to time and paid a high price for it. But there were other helpers, too, once such pair being the 'Undertaker' and his accomplice. It has been said that the Krays knew a bent funeral parlour director who disposed of dead bodies for them by putting the corpses into coffins with other bodies that were due to be buried [29]. Then there was the story doing the rounds that the bodies are propping up parts of the motorway. Nipper Read favoured the idea that the bodies were burnt in the furnace of a swimming baths opposite Vallance Road.

I don't blame anyone for putting false stories about, especially when it concerns the disposal of corpses. If I was in that position myself I would do exactly the same thing. It's a big thing to get rid of somebody else's evidence. But now I can reveal the truth as to where all the bodies went that were never found. Let's not forget that it was Reggie Kray's favourite saying, that if you didn't keep your mouth shut 'you'd disappear off the face of the earth'. He meant it, too, and this is the story how.

It all began when Germany invaded Poland at the start of WWII and thousands of Poles were put into concentration camps and murdered. Some Poles turned against their own people in order to save their own lives and went to work for the Nazis, helping them to burn the bodies of all the murdered. These people were knows as Kapos. When the Allies drove the Nazis out of Poland at the end of the War, a pair of Kapos escaped from one of the camps and made their way to England. To hide their secret past they split up, one going to live in South London while the other one settled in the East End. He could speak fluent English and so was able to take a job as a waiter in a very famous upmarket restaurant in the West End, which is still there today.

As the years passed, he opened a small café. He still kept in contact with his fellow Pole, who had by now set up home in Dartford, Kent.

The pair then went into partnership. They became well known in the criminal fraternity for buying stolen lorry loads of metal and breaking up stolen cars and selling the parts on the cheap. To help them in their work they had their own furnace built where they could melt down the metal and make their own ingots. Yet, despite the fact that they were a long way from Poland, their past finally caught up with them. One day another Polish criminal from South London drove to their place with a lorry to do business. When he went into the office he recognised them for who they were; he had been in the same concentration camp as them. To get him to keep his mouth shut, the two Poles made this man a silent partner in their business. I will call him John because he has since passed away and I would not like to cause grief to any member of his family.

I got to know John while I was in Wandsworth Prison in 1966. In those days Jews in prison all had a blue card put outside their cell to identify them as Jews. This was so that when the Jewish holidays began we could all be moved to one big hall in the prison, so as not to have any contact with the other cons. This is how I met John and we became very good friends. He told me about his boyhood in Poland and how his family had been killed by the Nazis. After the War his aunt and uncle got him to England and raised him as their own son.

In early 1968 I had my first heart attack and was given a single cell in prison. John was the first person to come and see me, bringing me some tobacco and food. When I found a letter in my cell one day telling me to keep my mouth shut to the police about my dealings with the Krays – especially why Ronnie Kray had branded me with red-hot pokers – John was the first person I poured out my heart to about what Ronnie had done to me (even though in my book, *Branded*, I wrote that the first two people I told were Scouse Terry – who the Twins had cut up and left needing 317 stitches – and his cellmate, Lofty).

John still had a year to serve but he told me that I had to do the right thing and put my children's lives first and talk to the police. Before he left my cell he wished me luck and gave me an address where I could get in touch with him when we were free. It was after I made a statement to the police and they had shipped me from Wandsworth Prison to the Eastchurch Open Prison on the Isle of Sheppy, that I was put under police protection. This lasted 14 months.

When the Kray trial was finally over I went to the West End and met up with my dear friend John. We were more like brothers than good friends. This was in 1969. John had settled up with his share of the business and together with the money he had saved it made him a wealthy man.

The last time I saw him he took me to the Hilton Hotel for a drink and that is when he told me that he was going to live in Australia. He asked me if I wanted to go out there and set up a business with him. I declined. That is when he poured out his heart to me. He told me that one day at the business premises he went to get something out of the freezer and got the shock of his life. As he rummaged inside he came across a dead body. When he confronted his partners about it they told him that they were being blackmailed and were being forced to get rid of the bodies for some of England's biggest gangsters. The Krays were mentioned.

John was told how they got rid of the bodies. First they put them into the freezer. When they were frozen, the bodies would then be cut up so that there was no blood. This was done on a bandsaw. They would then put the pieces into a furnace, to cremate the victim. John told me that this was the reason why he was going to live in Australia, to get away from those two wicked Polish bastards.

In the years ahead the police must have gathered some evidence about what happened. But when they did finally turn up at the site, it had disappeared. In its place was a large house, with a large pond in front.

And the Poles? They had disappeared.

This is a true story, and it's the one I favour as the method by which many of the Krays' victims were disposed of. I can't say all of them were got rid of this way, but some were. To my mind, it makes more sense than getting someone to drive a dead body all the way down to the coast and then getting them weighted and wrapped in chicken wire and given a burial at sea. There seems to be too much risk involved with that form of disposal.

I can't comment on what happened to Jack McVitie's body. All I know is that he was never found. Reggie Kray said while he was in prison that Jack was fish food. While completing this book I was told by a good friend of mine who was also a very good friend of the Twins that Jack McVitie's body was taken away by the two Kapos, who went to the church with a van and put trade plates on Jack's car and then towed it back to their business. This was where they cut up Jack's body on the bandsaw and threw the bits in the furnace.

Of course, so long as there is no body there will always be doubt. As a final footnote to the story, here is Charlie Kray's take on what happened to Jack, taken from the original 1976 text of his book, *Me And My Brothers*: 'There are experts in all trades and every walk of life whose names are well known even though they do not advertise. Among these experts are men who specialise in the removal of incriminating evidence... the bones of the late Mr McVitie are [not] shoring up a motorway, [nor is it true] that he provided fodder for a herd of pigs, that he was incinerated, chopped up or slipped into a coffin made for two. The remains of Jack McVitie, confined in a stout weighted sack, were dropped from an aircraft over the middle of the English Channel.'

CHAPTER 6

FRANK MITCHELL

'Well, do it bravely, and be secret,'
EDWARD II, BY CHRISTOPHER MARLOWE

Let me tell you a sad story now. I say that because I find Frank Mitchell's life story very depressing. He was no mad axeman. Not really. Again, that's just the story you've been fed over the years. However, very occasionally, you do hear about the real Frank Mitchell. It is important to report a little about the real Frank Mitchell here, and then relate his death at the hand of the Krays.

I knew Frank in my teenage years, and what I knew about him was that he was a bit slow in his thinking. What I also knew was that he wouldn't hurt an old person. He also loved children. Around the East End he was known as the gentle giant. Frank was 6ft 2in (2m). He came from a very good East End family and his only downfall was that he could be easily led by others.

When Frank first went to prison it was the warders –
screws, as the inmates call them – that took advantage of
Frank. Some of them were very brutal towards me, so I know
what they were like.

Frank Mitchell had been in and out of prison and mental
institutions most of his life. It was when Frank broke out of
Rampton Mental Institution that he started to attract a bit of
fame. Many stories have been told about how the police
captured Frank and none of them are true. It was said in the
papers that Frank was holding an old couple captive by
threatening them with an axe. Like so many other people, I
believed Frank would never do anything like that. We all
know how the truth can be twisted to make good reading –
an occupational hazard when it comes to anything to do with
the Krays. But let me tell you what I believe to be an accurate
account of Mitchell's arrest and his 'Mad Axeman' status.

The following story was told to me by one of the members
of the Firm who was minding Frank when he was being
hidden in the Barking flat by the Twins. First of all you've got
to understand the life that Frank was living at the time. He
had already been incarcerated in many different prisons and
mental institutions. He had at the same time been treated like
an animal by his captors. And with all the punishment that
they were putting him through, he took it like a man. That's
what he was: a man.

Frank escaped from Rampton and cut across some fields,
because the police cars were going around the lanes looking
for him. After a while he came across an old man that was
having difficulty chopping up parts of a tree trunk. So Frank,
being a strong man, took the axe from the man and started to

do the work for him. It was while he was swinging the axe down onto the logs that he was arrested. Frank went without a struggle, but from that day forward he was known as the 'Mad Axeman'.

Frank Mitchell was an icon of a man. A man among men. He took all the punishment that was dished out to him and he never complained once. He became a powerful and respected figure in prison because of the way he fought the system; even the screws came to respect him. No one could take Frank's dignity away from him and eventually Dartmoor became his final prison stop.

While on the Moor Frank began to buckle down and play by the rules. He always pined for a release date, but however much he yearned for one it didn't come. So he decided to rehabilitate himself and become a role-model prisoner. This earned him the status of Trusted Prisoner, which meant that he was allowed to work on an outside party on his own. By this time even the prison governor tried to get Frank a release date, but to no avail.

Frank had regular visits from friends and family, including the Kray twins. They always came in under assumed names, and that is how Frank came to idolise Ronnie Kray. He would believe anything that Ronnie told him, especially when he told Frank that he would get him out. Ronnie had first met Frank while serving a GBH sentence in Wandsworth Prison and it was from there that a friendship grew up between the two men [30].

During the weeks of planning Frank's escape from Dartmoor, the Twins would send two members of the Firm and a girl called Clare down to Dartmoor by car to find the easiest way back to London. The reason why they put a girl in the car was because it would take away any suspicion from them. She later became one of the witnesses at the Kray trial.

Finally, the day of Frank's escape came. Two of the Kray Firm drove down to Dartmoor with a change of clothes for Frank on the back seat [31]. They parked the car by the telephone box where they had arranged to pick Frank up. For a prisoner to escape unseen from a working party was almost an impossibility, but Mitchell was an amazing character. He reputedly used to be a regular at one of the local pubs, buying anyone a drink, made love to local girls and bought budgies!

A member of the Firm spent about 20 minutes inside the telephone box at the rendezvous point before Mitchell was spotted casually walking down the lane. As soon as Frank arrived and got in the car he changed his clothes [32]. By the time Frank was missed he was well on his way back to London. Apparently, all he kept asking about was when he would see Ronnie. By the time the police had set up their road blocks, Frank and his accomplices were back in London, residing in a safe flat in Barking Road.

After a few days Frank started to get a bit restless, so the Twins got him a girl to keep him quiet. She was a good-looking blonde called Lisa. Frank finally fell in love with her and for a long time they barely left the bedroom. Albert Donoghue and Billy Exley were left in the flat to look after Frank and Lisa and to see that they got everything they wanted. Reggie Kray would pay an occasional visit and whenever he did Frank kept asking when he was going to see Ronnie. It was clear to everyone that Frank was getting a bit anxious, feeling that he was more of a prisoner now than he ever was before. When the situation began to get out of hand and Frank started to become unstable, word got back to Reggie to come and see if he could sort things out.

Christmas was not far away and Frank was told that they were sending someone to pick him and Lisa up to take them down to the countryside to spend the festive season with Ronnie Kray [33]. Billy Exley told me that when Frank heard this he was over the moon. He was going to see his idol at last.

Albert and Billy were told that a car would come that very night to pick up the couple. But when a van pulled up outside Albert got a little suspicious. Once Frank got into the back of the van, Big Albert pulled Lisa back and told Frank that they would follow in another car. Albert knew the score. He knew that Frank's number was up. He had seen who else was in the back of the van: Freddie Foreman and Alfie Gerrard. Frank's angels of death had come [34].

Frank never did get to see his idol because he was shot dead by Alfie Gerrard. Albert's quick thinking had saved Lisa's life. Frank Mitchell was murdered less than a fortnight after his escape from Dartmoor on the request of the man who claimed to be his saviour, Ronnie Kray.

Lots of stories have been told about why the Krays got Frank out of prison. The only theory I can believe was told to me by a member of the Firm. He said that the Krays wanted Mitchell to kill Nipper Read because they knew that Nipper was putting together a case against them. When the Mitchell trial came up at the Old Bailey the whole thing was thrown out. The Krays had literally got away with murder. And as Frank's body was never found — a burial at sea courtesy of Freddie Foreman or a trip to the smelter? —

Frank's lovely family was never given the opportunity of allowing Frank a funeral.

Apparently, and I don't believe this, Reggie broke down and cried when he heard what had happened to Mitchell. Albert Donoghue said that, and I don't believe it because of what Albert related about me in his book, *The Enforcer*. Let me tell the story from the beginning, because it adds relevance to this chapter and highlights that the truth isn't always told about the Krays and the people who knew them – on this occasion, me.

Bobby Ramsey, an ex-pro boxer, was a minder on the door of the Kentucky Club along with Dougie King, and it was Ramsey that introduced the Krays to Jack Spot. Anyway, Albert mentioned in his book that I was a little worried around that time that I would upset the Twins about something or other. I phoned them up to square it and that night Ronnie told an ex-wrestler called Andy Paul, who was living with me, to get me to go to Esmeralda's Barn, where he would meet me. Andy woke me at about 1:00 a.m. with this news and I got up and took a taxi to the Barn.

Donoghue relates in his book that when I got there I tried to escape, but was taken into the kitchen and tied to a chair. Despite being branded with red-hot pokers, I then signed on with the Krays. I can tell you now that that is a load of lies. I never signed on with the Krays, ever.

Then Donoghue goes further in his book, stating that I was the reason why he got shot in the leg by Reggie. Donoghue relates that the next time he saw me after the shooting was when he came into a pub I was drinking in and asked me for money for his Away List. He states that I tried to give him a fiver, so Donoghue apparently said: 'You're not getting away with that you little rat, I want some more.' According to Donoghue I then gave him £25, which upset me because I couldn't then buy a drink after that. He then says that this was just his way of getting revenge on me for his being shot.

The Away List? What the fuck was the Away List! It's all lies. But people believe those lies because they are told by somebody who was there.

I personally have never heard of the Away List, and to put the record straight he never asked me for money. In those days, if someone had just come out of the nick and you were holding money you would give them a few quid to help them out. I have been treated in the same way myself.

So here you have a different version of what went on. And this is not just my version of events. As you read this book you will also read the stories of Eric Mason, Billy Frost and others. We've all got together to put together our memories to tell you the truth. The full truth as we see it in the East End.

CHAPTER 7
TEDDY SMITH

'As for Teddy Smith, he just disappeared off the face of the earth and yet he was the guy who drove Mitchell off the Moor... everybody was saying the same thing, "Teddy Smith is a goner," but the where and the why for?'
NIPPER READ

Ask Nipper Read if the Krays killed Teddy Smith and he would say: 'I have no idea. I've tried to look at that as narrowly as possible and I have no idea' [35]. It is clear to many people that if Nipper Read had to attempt to get the Krays on another murder charge after Mitchell it probably would have been that of 'Mad' Teddy Smith.

Teddy Smith was a member of the Kray Firm. He was closer to Ronnie Kray than to Reggie, probably because they were both openly homosexual. Teddy was a very clever man who wrote plays and scripts for television. He was far from being mad, as he was described by the newspapers.

Teddy was a good-looking man, with dark, curly hair. He was also the lover of a member of parliament. Teddy was one of the two men that helped Frank Mitchell escape from Dartmoor, as I will mention later on in this chapter.

The first time that I met Teddy was when I was having a drink in the Kismet Club, which belonged to a woman called Maltese Mary. I was in the company of Susan Shaws, the film star, who was a very good friend of mine. Teddy also knew Susan because of all the television people he used to go around with.

Teddy came into the bar with some friends of his, all smartly dressed. I knew from experience what type of people they were. I'm not against homosexuals, so I had a few drinks with them and then left. After that, I would often see Teddy in the drinking clubs around the West End and I enjoyed his company. I also occasionally had a drink with him in the Regency Club. I knew that Teddy was on the Kray Firm, but that did not bother me because he had never done anything to me.

He was a generous man, and good company until the drink started to get to him. On one occasion I was having a drink in a pub in Highgate Village called The Flask and, of all people, who should walk in but Teddy Smith. We had a few drinks together and a few laughs because Teddy had a very good sense of humour. As the conversation went on, he said to me: 'Len, what do you think of them two idiots?' (meaning the Kray Twins). I knew who he was talking about straight away, but I let him think that I didn't understand. Teddy went on and told me that he was up in the West End a few nights previously and had a row in one of the clubs. The next day the Krays sent a driver to pick him up and take him to their house. He told me that the Twins had a go at him for causing trouble in one of the clubs that they were receiving protection money from. I half smiled because I could see the funny side of it. But Teddy wasn't smiling when he said: 'Who the fuck do that pair of fucking queer bastards think they are talking to?'

It didn't appear to be a question. Teddy was getting upset and a little bit drunk, so I made my excuses and left. Teddy was like Jack McVitie when he was drunk. He would go into one, not unlike a lot of other people, I'm sure. But the truth is, the Twins were really getting the hump with him because he was getting drunk around the clubs that they had an interest in. The club owners knew that Teddy was a member of the Kray Firm. Besides that, it was beginning to look like the Krays had no control over their Firm with Teddy misbehaving. So once again he was cautioned by the Twins for his drunkenness and told to stay away from any of the clubs that they were getting protection money from. Teddy respected their word and stayed away from the West End.

The last time I saw Teddy was in the Regency Club, where some of the Kray Firm went.

I was told by someone on the Firm that Teddy had been up to his old tricks, getting drunk and telling people how he got Frank Mitchell out of Dartmoor. Word soon got back to the Twins about this, and they had the word put about that Teddy had left the country and gone to live in Australia. If that is true, why did Reggie take a good friend of mine round to Teddy's house and remove Teddy's car so that none of the neighbours would get suspicious? Then why did Reggie have Teddy's car taken to a scrap yard and have it crushed?

I found out that it was Reggie Kray who killed Teddy Smith. He may well have gone down under, but not to Australia. Six feet under, more like, after Reggie Kray shot him in the back of the head up a little alleyway. And that's the truth.

Teddy Smith did a lot for the Twins. He caused some damage in Hew McCowan's club, which led to a court case. He was a known homosexual who appeared in some of the photographs of Ronnie Kray and Lord Boothby, the famous 'Peer and the Gangster' picture especially. Johnny Squibb, another friend of the Krays, apparently sold this photograph to the newspapers, which means it was probably just another scam put together by the Firm.

Teddy Smith was also a Kray confidant. He was the guy who drove Mitchell off the Moor and before that wrote Mitchell's letters to the newspapers requesting a release date. In fact, he knew every aspect of the Frank Mitchell murder from start to finish. With hindsight, had he been around at the time of the Twins' arrest he would have been a perfect witness.

But Teddy Smith wasn't around. He was dead. He probably went to Dartford, where he was frozen, cut up on the bandsaw and put into the furnace. So the Kray twins' villainy went on, and up to that point they *were* getting away with murder. But that said, they never had the guts to clean up the mess that they left behind when they committed their murders. They had to involve other members of their Firm in that. All this goes to show how much power the Krays had over the Firm. Not all the members of the Firm were bad people. They just had to do what they were told or else they would have to suffer the consequences. I know that quite a few of the Firm wanted to get away from the Twins, but because they knew too much they had no option but to stay. Then, as well as the Firm members, there were also a lot of fringe people who enjoyed being lackeys for Ronnie and Reggie, just to be in their good books. The four I disliked most of all were Billy Ackerman, Sammy Lederman, Harry Jew Boy and, most of all, Tony Lambrianou.

I have done my share of time in prison, and anyone that has been inside has got to admire the two men that would never bow down to the prison system: Frank Mitchell and Frankie Fraser. If you've not been in prison it's hard to imagine what someone like Fraser had to go through while he was serving out his 42 years of incarceration. When I was serving my prison sentences in the 1950s and 1960s, the cons would get beaten up and no questions were asked.

In those days, there was so much brutality going on in the prisons that it's no wonder some of the cons were volatile – I hit a ginger-headed screw when I was in Pentonville. I was put on report for that and got 14 days bread and water and a loss of 28 days remission. I was also put in the chokey block where, from time to time, the screws would come into your cell and give you a right going over. I was beaten up so badly on one occasion that when the prison medical officer came into my cell to treat me for my wounds he was shocked to see me in such a state. After he had patched me up he said to the screw on duty that this type of brutality had to stop. But it still went on.

I don't condone the violence that Fraser inflicted on some people because violence is his way of life. To be honest, I think that he is another Ronnie Kray, getting pleasure out of seeing someone in pain. But with all his faults he would not stand any nonsense from a prison screw or even the prison governor. Fraser fought the prison system. Although they treated him like some kind of animal, they could not break him – and for that he had to suffer in the many different prisons he was in. Nevertheless, he always came out on top. Today, after all the violence and the prison terms, Frankie Fraser is a household name.

When I was in Wandsworth Prison I got on friendly terms with another con who came out of the Elephant and Castle, south of the river. His name was Mickey Rolf. He was a very nice man who would do you a favour if he could. I heard that he is a very rich man now and I say good luck to him. We did time in the chokey together, and even Mickey would stand no nonsense from the screws.

In those days prison life was hard because the food was bloody awful. The porridge was grade one pigs' food, full of lumps. The bread ration was measly and you were given a tin knife and fork to eat with. When you had finished your day's work in one of the prison workshops you were then given a cell task. If you failed to carry it out you were put on report and lost remission, and did some time in chokey (solitary confinement) as well.

While I was in Wandsworth, the governor was Mr Charles Lawton, a very hard man who would instinctively believe his officers over the cons. I relate all of this because it puts the reader into the prison mindset of yesteryear. The prison system has changed so much over the past 40 years. Gone is the red light in the cell that stayed on all through the night. In prisons today there are light switches, so that cons can turn the lights on and off as they wish. You can also wear your own clothes inside now. No wonder some old cons call prison Butlin's Holiday Camp nowadays.

I did not make many friends while I was in prison because you had so many grasses in there. You had to watch who you spoke to as they would grass you up to the screws in return for special favours from them. My personal experience of prison life is that in no way did it rehabilitate me. To my mind, rehabilitation has to come from within. If you don't look deep inside yourself you will be in and out of prison for the rest of your life. The times that I have spent in prison, I have seen some of the same old faces again and again.

One thing that people say today is that crime is different now, that it is much worse and that it affects more of the general public. This may be true in some cases, but not all. I have been in pubs and markets around the East End and I have been pulled up by people who told me that if the Krays were around today we would not have a drug problem, that they would have stopped it. I can't agree with that. If that is the case, why was it that the Twins had a chemist in a small workshop in Essex turning out purple hearts in the early 1960s? And why did they send Jack McVitie round the East End pubs and West End clubs to try and sell them on? They also had people going round the local dance halls selling them. Jack would take some of the pills himself and, by his own admission to me, he had become addicted to them. The

Krays were having these pills turned out by the thousand, and they were flooding the whole of the East End and West End with them.

The Twins didn't care where their money came from, just as long as it kept rolling in. I believe that if they were alive today they would be the biggest drug dealers in the country, because they liked the colour of money and had all the right connections to dispose of the product of that evil trade.

I then hear people say that if the Krays were still around there would be no muggings and street crime. I would like to point out that muggings have only got so bad in the last ten years as most of them are caused by young kids on drugs and by youths from ethnic minorities – the very people who would not care about or respect the Krays.

The Krays survived through the fear that they instilled in people. I have seen what fear can do to people because I have been in that situation myself when Ronnie burnt me. I had nightmares for quite a long time afterwards. I am 74 years of age at the time of writing, but if I had known then what I know now I would have gone and got a gun and shot that evil bastard Ronnie Kray. Like every one of us, gangsters are not invincible. They too can die.

I was in prison when the Twins threatened to kill my two children. In order for me to get police protection for my kids I had to sign a statement naming Ronnie Kray as the person that tortured me. I would do the same thing again if my family was put in the same situation. I knew that by going against the Krays I was putting my own life at risk, but my family had to come first. Looking back at the disappeared, the

Frank Mitchells and Teddy Smiths of this world, I'm pleased that I did. Some people may disagree but they were never in my situation. And I hope for their sakes that they never are.

CHAPTER 8

FRANCES SHEA

'He lowered the pistol to her chest. For the few moments the gun had been pointed at her head, she believed he'd just been trying to scare her, make her shit her pants or beg forgiveness and climb into the limo. Now, she knew.'

SOULS TO KEEP, BY DAVID L ROBBINS

In the mid-1960s a young and very good-looking man joined the Kray Firm as Reggie's driver. His name was Frankie Shea. Frankie lived with his parents and his beautiful younger sister, Frances, in Ormsby Street, Bethnal Green.

The Sheas were well liked by their local community and Frances would turn the head of many a man with her stunning beauty. She was the talk of Bethnal Green. It was because of Frankie that Reggie first set eyes on her; they were not childhood sweethearts as is sometimes stated.

If one cares to find a copy of *The East End Advertiser*, dated Thursday, 18 January 2002, there is a short piece on page three by Frankie Shea, entitled: 'I SPURNED GAY REG KRAY SO HE WED MY SISTER IN REVENGE'. The story, written by Frankie, vindicates what I'm about to tell you: Reggie was in love with Frankie Shea, not Frances Shea.

When Frankie started working for Reggie, it quickly became clear that Reggie would have nobody else drive him. No matter what, Frankie had to drive him. Frankie soon worked out that Reggie fancied him. But Frankie wasn't gay, far from it, so he left the Firm. To get his own back on Frankie, Reggie found out where Frances worked and waited in his car for her to come out. She wasn't won over by him straight away, but Reggie bought her all sorts of presents and she finally gave in and went out on a date with him – not knowing how Reggie felt about her brother.

After leaving the Firm Frankie found himself a flat in North London, far away from the Krays' clutches. In the meantime, Reggie had only taken Frances out a few times before he asked her to marry him [36]. When Frances told her mother and father they couldn't believe it. They didn't want their lovely daughter married to a gangster. Even Frances was opposed to the idea. She liked her job and told Reggie that she thought that she was too young to get married. To win Frances over Reggie threatened to kill her father and her brother. Faced with this, Frances gave in.

Reggie married Frances on 19 April 1965 at St James the Great Church in Bethnal Green. Ronnie Kray was the best man and David Bailey was the official photographer. The media dubbed it The East End Wedding of the Year. Mrs Shea for one didn't see it that way. She arrived at the church dressed in black, to show her contempt towards Reggie. The whole marriage was a sham right from the start and after just six weeks – including a Mediterranean honeymoon – Frances left Reggie and returned home to her parents.

Reggie was having none of that. Every night he would go round to the Sheas' house and, as Mr and Mrs Shea wouldn't let him in, Frances would speak to Reggie from the bedroom window. Frances wasn't silly. She knew that the strain of Reggie's daily visits was telling on her parents. To stop it she finally agreed to go back to him.

Reggie had rented a furnished flat in Lancaster Gate and, as the weeks went by, Frances became a grass widow as Reggie and Ronnie still had their nights out in the clubs around the West End and poor Frances was left in the flat on her own. Ronnie Kray had taken a flat in Cedra Court in North London and when the flat below his became vacant Reggie and Frances moved in.

Things did not change for Frances in the new flat because Reggie would not let her go out by herself. He would occasionally take her to a club in the West End, but that was only to make people think that they had a good marriage. Ronnie was happy when Reggie and Frances moved to Cedra Court, because it meant that he was closer to his twin brother. He would enjoy going up to the Astor Club with Reggie, then returning to his flat for more drinks with some young gay boys.

While this was all going on, Frances would be in the flat below, locked in her bedroom and out cold from the tablets that the Twins would force down her throat to make her sleep. They would also leave a member of the Firm in the flat to ensure that she didn't stir.

One night, they got my friend Billy Exley to look after Frances. I knew Billy very well. He was a good man who wanted to get away from the Krays, but he knew too much and they wouldn't let him go. In fact, Billy and I became good friends because I saved his life back in the early 1960s; but that's a different story.

So, Billy was locked in the flat with a drugged-up Frances when, in the early hours of the morning, Reggie came in blind drunk with a hostess that he had picked up from one of the clubs. The next morning, Frances woke up to find Reggie lying next to her and next to *him* was the hostess. Billy told me that Frances started screaming for her mum. Ronnie came down from his flat and got the hostess out of the flat and Frances ran to get out, too. Ronnie pulled her back by her hair calling her a 'fucking old slag'. After it all calmed down, Ronnie asked Billy Exley: 'What the fuck were you doing while all this was going on?' Exley replied, quite calmly, that it was a domestic squabble and that it was none of his business to interfere. Ronnie's answer to that was: 'Alright Billy, you have made your point, and you did the right thing.' The one thing I can say about Ronnie Kray is that you were safe if you were telling him the truth. The one thing that Ronnie could not stand was a liar.

As he made his way out of the flat, Ronnie told Billy to make sure Reggie got back into bed, because he was still drunk and had fallen asleep on the settee. Billy finally got Reggie back into bed, making sure that he was fast asleep before he let Frances out of the flat. When Reggie woke up, Billy pretended to be asleep on the settee. Reggie started shaking Billy and demanded to know where Frances was.

Billy feigned innocence and told Reggie that he thought she had been in bed with him. Reggie lost his temper and started calling Billy all the names under the sun, eventually telling him to 'fuck off out and find Frances'.

Billy later told me that he had no intention of finding Frances, so he went home. Frances had gone back to her parents' house and swore that she would have nothing more to do with Reggie. From that day she changed her name back to Frances Shea. But all of this was telling on the poor girl. She became clinically depressed and was admitted to Hackney Hospital. She was quickly discharged but the problems didn't go away and she was eventually admitted into a nursing home in Camden Town. Again, she was later discharged.

A couple of days after Frances' discharge Reggie started going back round to the Sheas' house and demanding to see his wife. Mrs Shea told him that she had had enough of his threats and told him that if he didn't stop coming round she would call the police. But Reggie carried on coming and so Frances moved out again, this time going to stay with her brother Frankie in Wimbourne Court, Hoxton.

It is hard to imagine the torment that Frances went through. She was ridiculed and abused by the Krays until finally she could take no more. She waited until she knew that her brother Frankie was going out for while and then took an overdose, falling into a deep sleep from which she would never wake.

Frankie only discovered his beautiful sister's body the next morning, when he went to wake her up. The empty pill phials scattered across her bed confirmed his worst fears. The date was 7 June 1967. The post-mortem stated that Frances died of a massive overdose of phenobarbitone, which had been taken sometime during the night. The coroner's recorded verdict was of 'suicide while the balance of mind was disturbed'.

This is the sad truth about Reggie Kray's marriage to Frances Shea.

It has been often said that when Frances died, Reggie couldn't get over her. That he began to drink heavily. That's not true. Reggie was a heavy drinker before Frances took her life. However, because of his own guilt, Reggie did start looking for sympathy.

It has been said that Reggie didn't know how to hold a woman. Well, he didn't do bad with all the other women he slept with, such as the hostess, or even the woman who had his son. But it was also confirmed by the coroner's report that Frances Shea died a virgin. Reggie played his part very well. In fact, he should have got an Oscar for his performance. He never consummated his marriage to Frances and, after France's death, her mother fought to get the marriage annulled.

Reggie Kray only married Frances Shea to get his own back on her brother Frankie, and to hide the fact that he was bisexual.

The Twins killed that girl as sure as if they had put a gun to her head and pulled the trigger. And that's another side to their evil. They didn't simply shoot people, they tormented them, playing with them like a cat with a mouse. Looking back at Reggie and Frances' relationship, that's exactly what it was like. Reggie was the sly cat and poor Frances was the startled mouse. And what about Frances' parents? They had to live with the grief of losing a daughter in her early 20s. They blamed the Krays for making Frances suicidal and there is also speculation that Reggie introduced Frances to drugs. Indeed, in his book, *The Cult Of Violence*, John Pearson claimed that Reggie gave Frances drugs obtained from the quack, Dr Blasker, who supplied Ronnie Kray with drugs to calm his schizophrenia. It is speculated that these drugs more or less resulted in Frances having a nervous breakdown.

When Frances was buried Reggie wanted her to wear her wedding dress, but her mother ensured that Frances wore something underneath it so that no part of the dress touched her skin. Also, Frances' mother managed to switch the ring on her finger from Reggie's wedding ring to one that she had given her daughter. That's how strongly Frances' parents felt about their daughter's relationship with Reggie Kray. As for her brother, he was later prepared to go into print in his local newspaper to explain how Reggie Kray felt about him. It only took him so long to do this as he did not want his mother to read about it all. He waited until she died until he published the story.

Frances was a lovely girl. Shy, innocent and wholesome. My heart goes out to the Shea family for the evil that infected their lives and resulted in the loss of that poor girl. Sadly, her final resting place is beside Reggie Kray in the Kray plot at Chingford Cemetery.

CHAPTER 9

THE RENT BOY

'That's what the Kray world was all about – a frightening madness of murder and mayhem from which, for me, there seemed no escape.'

ESCAPE FROM THE KRAY MADNESS, BY CHRIS LAMBRIANOU

It is a well-known fact that Ronnie Kray was gay. When he told his elder brother, Charlie was amazed. 'I can't believe it, mate,' he apparently said. But Ronnie Kray was quite upfront about it and said: 'Mum knows and it's alright with her, so it's alright with you.'

Ronnie had boyfriends throughout his younger life. This is known fact. What isn't so well known is that Ronnie Kray once fell in love with a rent boy and eventually killed him.

Ronnie met the young, fair-haired lad one night in the West End. After paying for his services a few times, Ronnie fell in love with him.

GETTING AWAY WITH MURDER

I must give Ronnie Kray his due. He took the boy off the streets and set him up in a flat in the West End. Ronnie paid the rent and bought the young man clothes and jewellery and, to be honest, as mad as he was, he always treated his lover well. That was until he found out the boy had been cheating on him. Finding this out made his paranoia worse and he made it his quest to teach his lover a lesson.

Ronnie arranged to go away for the weekend to their caravan in Steeple Bay, Essex. On the day they were due to depart, Ronnie sent a driver to pick up the young man and bring him back to his mum's house in Vallance Road. When the driver arrived, Reggie got in the front seat next to the driver, while Ronnie climbed in the back with his boyfriend.

On the way to the caravan Ronnie started to get a bit drunk on the odd gin and tonic. He then started to slap the young lad around, calling him all the filthy names under the sun. Reggie told Ronnie to stop hitting the boy because he would get them nicked. When they finally arrived at their destination and they were inside the caravan, Ronnie started to get even more aggressive towards the lad. Naturally, the boy ran towards Reggie and the driver for protection. But Ronnie was now firmly in one of his moods. No one knew what he would do next when he was in that dark state.

On this occasion, Ronnie slowly strangled the lad. The driver stood there in shock, not daring to move. If he had, he could easily have become the next victim.

Once Ronnie had quietened down, he and Reggie wrapped the boy in some bed sheets and put him in the boot of the car. They then got the driver to take the body back to

London and told him to keep his mouth shut – otherwise he would end up in the boot, too.

That's how unpredictable Ronnie Kray was. He enjoyed seeing people in pain, no matter what the cost. The story of Mickey Morris is not dissimilar to that of the rent boy and shows again the callousness and blood-lust of the Kray twins.

Mickey was an East End boy. Very good-looking and also a good thief. I enjoyed many a drink in his company and enjoyed his friendship until he started to get about with the Kray twins. Then, for some unknown reason, the Twins got the needle with Mickey. They decided to deal with him and arranged a party upstairs in the Widows pub, with the whole Firm invited. Everyone turned up and began to enjoy themselves. Ronnie and Reggie were sitting on a settee, half drunk, when Mickey walked into the room. The Twins invited him to sit with them, and no sooner had he sat down than Reggie pulled out a knife and stabbed Mickey through the shoulder while Ronnie was punching him. As Mickey sat there losing a lot of blood Reggie went into the kitchen and calmly washed the blood from the knife, placing it back in his pocket. Then, as if nothing had happened, they all left, except one member of the Firm who took Mickey to hospital. The police were called and the Kray Firm member was questioned. He told the police that he was on his way home when he saw two black men having a fight with Mickey and that when they saw him coming they ran off, leaving their victim on the floor covered in blood.

Mickey was rushed into the emergency theatre to have a blood transfusion to replace what he had lost. The Firm member was thanked by the police and by a doctor, who told him that he had just saved Mickey's life.

Mickey recovered from his ordeal and stayed well away from the Krays after that. He died from natural causes some time later, but I remained a friend of his until the end.

CHAPTER 10

THE STRANGE CASE OF DR BLASKER AND MR KRAY

'Between these two I now had to choose. My two natures had memory in common, but all other facilities were most unequally shared between them.'
STRANGE CASE OF DR JEKYLL AND MR HYDE,
ROBERT LOUIS STEVENSON

What follows isn't a Kray murder story. However, it does explain an awful lot about the Twins' state of mind during their heyday and how they got their hands on certain drugs when needed – drugs which certainly affected their behaviour.

This story isn't a revelation. It has been mentioned in other Kray books, but if the intention of this book is to present new information concerning Kray murders then it is important to detail what contributed to the Krays' mind-set when committing those murders. This makes for a more complete and realistic picture of events. So here is the strange case of Dr Blasker and Mr Kray.

Ronnie Kray was known as 'The Colonel' and his parents' home of 178 Vallance Road was known as 'Fort Vallance'. And it really was a fortress, filled with weapons hidden there by Ronnie. In fact, Ronnie had a thing about hiding firearms in his various safe houses and stores. It made him feel very secure.

In his mind Ronnie Kray was a military leader and the Firm were his soldiers. As far as Ronnie was concerned, he was conducting a war and this meant that any form of violence was justified. His mind wasn't normal. He was – as he and his family eventually found out – a paranoid schizophrenic [37]. This is a highly dangerous illness, which if not carefully treated results in the individual becoming extremely violent – which Ronnie Kray was most of the time.

Let's not blame everything on Ronnie alone. Reggie was a cold and violent man – more so after a few drinks (see Billy Frost interview at Annexe B). Nipper Read said in December 2001: 'They were desperately villainous people. Cruel and wicked and merciless. They enjoyed inflicting pain for the sheer pleasure of it.' Reggie and Ronnie shared the same thoughts, feelings and lack of emotion. They were two peas in a pod, or, more accurately, the same egg divided. They were twins and the power of that relationship cannot be underestimated.

On 20 February 1958 Ronnie Kray was diagnosed as suffering from schizophrenia. He left hospital on 18 November that same year, having received treatment for his condition continually throughout that time. However, from that time on until his long-term return to prison in 1968 Ronnie received drugs and treatment for his illness from an East End doctor named Dr Blasker, a quack if ever there was one.

The drugs would – on the admission of certain members of the Kray Firm – turn Ronnie from a raving lunatic into a zombie. It was clear that Blasker was over-medicating Ronnie, but with what? No one even knows if he was giving Ronnie the right sort of pills to help him properly.

In his periods in prison Ronnie was usually prescribed with the right sort of medication and was consequently relatively well behaved. But outside of jail he was capable of anything, as this following incident that took place at the Central Club in Clerkenwell shows. Ronnie was having a drink with a friendly Italian by the name of Battles. During the evening Battles had an argument with a man called Billy Alco. Things eventually calmed down, but later than night Ronnie saw Alco and a friend talking and looking over at him. Ronnie Kray explained what happened next in *Our Story*: 'That did it. I was convinced Alco and his mates were plotting against me.' This is how the mind of a paranoid schizophrenic works without medication. Ronnie continued: 'I had a revolver on me at the time and I took it out and had a shot at Alco. Luckily I missed, but the shot caused fucking chaos in the club. I was ready to shoot them all, but Battles held my arm and said to me very quietly, "It's not necessary, Ron, let's go." Something in the way he said it brought me to my senses and we left.'

From December 1968 Ronnie Kray was prescribed 25

milligrams of Stemetil, to be taken three times a day. By his own admission he preferred to take it four times a day. This implies that, given the opportunity, he would gladly take more of the drug to avoid getting 'depressed'.

All of this suggests that Blasker perhaps assisted Ronnie to curb his day-to-day violent outbursts, but there is more to it than that. Blasker gave the Twins whatever they wanted in the way of 'medication'. Ronnie would get properly prescribed medication from time to time, but Blasker was a useful tool, especially when obtaining extra medication for Reggie's wife Frances, who supposedly suffered from suicidal tendencies.

With regard to Reggie's medication, it appears from documents in the National Archive that he took five milligrams of valium three time a day. It was properly and lawfully prescribed to him by Dr Lewis Clein, Frances Shea's psychiatrist, so a genuine source of medication is sourced here. Of course, while they were covering their backs by receiving medication through official channels such as this, the Twins were also obtaining drugs from characters like Blasker. In addition, they were also running their own drug-making factory in Essex, churning out the purple hearts that Jack McVitie and others peddled around London's pubs and clubs.

There is evidence and witnesses to back up the claim that the Krays dabbled in soft drugs from the turn of the 1950s, which was quite early for the British underworld. In his book, *Ronnie Kray – A Man Amongst Men*, Laurie O'Leary stated that the Krays never dabbled in drugs. Well, they didn't dabble openly and drugs were not central to the Firm's activities, but drugs were there. Laurie O'Leary was never a crook and was a genuine friend of the Twins. His book is a testament to that fact and fully details their early years, when they were only as bad as any other tough East End lads. However, it was in the Twins' latter years that the drugs came into things. This was when Dr Blasker became a more important part of their lives.

In his book, *The Profession Of Violence*, John Pearson writes: 'Most schizophrenics find it hard to face the world and finally collapse through inability to reconcile their delusions with the world outside. The paranoid schizophrenic is different. Even if he has a breakdown, his obsession can persist despite it' [38]. Many people would agree that Ronnie Kray spent too long without receiving proper treatment for his illness. I'm not creating excuses for Ronnie; this is merely a comment on a society that is meant to protect the public. There are so many dangerous people on the streets, people with mental problems whose main agenda in life is to hurt others. Every year there is at least one big murder or rape committed by someone suffering from mental illness yet society never seems to wise up and protect itself. It's not survival of the fittest; it's survival of the weirdest, or cruellest. You're not fit if you're mentally unwell or taking drugs, and you're certainly not fit if you need to carry a weapon.

As for Ronnie Kray, his mental health problems were well known, yet he was allowed to rampage around the East End from 1958 to 1968. Where's the support for people like that today; where's the protection for the general public?

CHAPTER 11

THE ONES THAT GOT AWAY

'I've shot several people over the years,'
My Story, by Ronnie Kray

Despite the Krays' best efforts, some people managed to survive their tyranny – even after having a gun fired at them from point-blank range.

If you really want to know more about the cavalier attitude to friendship, disloyalty and death that the Kray twins had, it is important to detail the people who managed to somehow escape from their clutches. This brings greater perspective to the characters of the people the Krays did kill. It also brings greater perspective to what people say about those victims and, ostensibly, the perception of the Krays by the people who only know them through books written by or about them.

What I really want to get across is the fact that the murders were senseless killings, just as Nipper Read has described them. I don't want you to look at Jack McVitie and George

Cornell's photographs in Kray books and say to yourself that these were people who lived by the sword and died by the sword because they didn't. Yes, they came from a tough area but they weren't bad people. So, let us look at those who are not usually included in the Kray statistics and see what type of people they are. Perhaps then you'll understand more about the Krays and their victims.

In his books, *Our Story* and *My Story*, Ronnie was never very forthcoming about the people he shot. But he does give a vivid account of the first person he ever raised a firearm in anger to. He wrote: 'The first person I shot was an ex-boxer called Shorty, who was trying to put the squeeze for protection money on a friend of ours who owned a garage. Shorty didn't know this feller was a friend of ours, of course. When Shorty went to the garage to collect his money, he found me there waiting for him. He started to get lippy, made a couple of threats, so I shot him in the leg with an automatic Luger. The police arrested me and put me on an identification parade, but Shorty wasn't stupid and he didn't pick me out.' If this all sounds blasé and matter-of-fact that's because it is. Ronnie Kray shot people. It wasn't such a big deal to him.

To keep this chapter as authentic as possible I want to spend a little time talking about the Dixons – especially George Dixon, who nearly lost his life to Ronnie Kray. A lot has been said about George and Alan Dixon – mostly by people that never knew them – so I want to talk about them from my perspective as someone who really did know the brothers.

Alan and George came from a nice family that lived in Canning Town. They were two very tall men and they were also very powerful. They could hold their hands up to anyone. George was probably the more laid back and reserved, whereas Alan was always the one up for a laugh. Alan also had a lovely voice and when he sang around some of the pubs in the East End you could see some of the young girls going all starry eyed, because he did have a great voice.

I have known the Dixons since the early 1950s and I can, with all honesty, say that in all that time I have never heard or seen them take a liberty with anyone.

George and Alan had a friend named Philly Jacobs, who was the governor of a pub called the Bridge House in Canning Town. George and Alan were the minders in the pub and their job was to keep any troublemakers out, which they did very well. Being that they were both over 6ft (2m) few people would take them on. If anyone did have a go at them, they rarely did it twice. The Dixons kept the bad apples out of the pub and people in the East End respected them for that. I'd been in their company around the East End and I never saw them cause any trouble. In fact, they were more like peacemakers and would always try to stop a fight. But every now and again they would come up against some flash bastard out to make a name for himself. The result being that the flash bastard always came unstuck.

Philly Jacobs took over a larger pub in Leytonstone High Street, called the Plough and Harrow. George and Alan Dixon went with him as pub minders and they did a terrific job of keeping all the troublemakers away. People knew that they could go into the Plough and Harrow and be able to enjoy their drinks and have a good night out in safety, courtesy of the Dixon brothers.

One night, in the Green Dragon in Aldgate, I was sitting at one of the tables making a book playing double pack rummy. Because I was making the book I would give the other three players 11/4 odds for any amount of money that they cared to gamble. George and Alan came in to enjoy a game of cards on what was just an ordinary night in the Green Dragon. Each table had their players and George and Alan were soon sitting down and trying their luck. Then everything changed when the Kray twins walked in.

I could see that the Twins were both a little the worse the wear for drink. When Ronnie Kray passed our table, like everyone else I thought that he had gone into the toilet to relieve himself. But when he came out he was holding a gun and he walked up to the table where George Dixon was sitting and put the gun to George's head. By this time, men were hiding under the tables or locking themselves in the toilet. It was like a Western. I even saw a couple of blokes jump out the window into Dragon Green Yard to get away. When Ronnie pulled the trigger the only noise that could be heard was a click. Ronnie Kray had another try but the gun was jammed. And that's what saved George's life that night. To tell you the truth, to this day I still don't know why that maniac would threaten George. I was told that someone had been winding up Ronnie Kray in the pub. I guess it was someone that had the needle with George but never had the guts to front the man himself.

Since those days George has really done well for himself and met and married a very nice girl. Her father ran the Morgan Arms pub in Coburn Road, Bow, and if my memory serves me well her name was Sheila. George was always a businessman and since the 1960s has owned a holiday hotel in Clacton-on-Sea. He has also owned hotels in some of the Kent seaside resorts and people I know who have stayed in his hotels can only give him a good name.

We have all come a long way since the 1960s. As for George Dixon, with hard work and a good wife by his side he has become a millionaire and now lives abroad. Alan Dixon lives in Essex. Although he is in ill health Alan keeps in touch with me by phone. His is a friendship I cherish.

The Dixons were always well dressed and polite. Every time I met Alan he would always shake my hand and kiss me on the cheek, which was his custom with his friends. Some people tried to make out that the Dixons were hardened criminals and that they tried to take over in the East End when the Krays were sent down. That's not true. The Dixons were shoulder to shoulder with the shopkeepers, publicans and business people who stood their ground after the Krays' conviction to put an end to the protection rackets that plagued the East End. It's now a thing of the past and I sincerely hope it stays that way. All I know is that a lot of people were jealous to see the Dixons getting on in life. As the old saying goes, you can't please all of the people all of the time. I was privileged to know George and Alan and to be considered their friend. They are two good cockney boys, one of whom was nearly killed for no good reason by that lunatic Ronnie Kray.

George Dixon just happened to encounter Ronnie Kray on a bad day. As Ronnie himself wrote in *My Story*: 'A feller called George Dixon upset me in a club and I tried to kill him. I took out my Luger, aimed it at his head and pulled the trigger. Dixon was lucky because the gun jammed. He run out of the club fucking quickly. It must have been a million to one against the gun jamming. Later I made friends with Dixon and gave him the bullet. I thought it would be a good reminder to him to be careful about who he upset.' There you have a perfect example of the way that Ronnie Kray's brain worked. One moment he would be against you and the next he would be apologetic for the pain and disfigurement he caused you.

I want to end this chapter on a lighter note, to give an example of another one that got away – but this time it was thanks to one of the Krays' victims.

I have been friends with this guy for some years now and always found him to be a real nice guy. He was in the Whisky-A-Go-Go Club in Wardour Street, Soho, one night when he got himself into a fight with another character, which ended with my friend stabbing him.

The man he stabbed was a friend of the Krays and when Reggie heard about the fight he was enjoying a drink in the Widows pub. He put the word out that if anyone came across my friend they were to ask him to come and see Reggie for a drink. Everyone knew what that meant.

A couple of weeks later Reggie went to a party in Tottenham when who should turn up but my friend. When Reggie saw him, he went to the bathroom and came out holding a gun wrapped in a towel. This man knew that Reggie had been looking for him over the fight, so when he saw Reggie coming up behind him in the hallway he decided to get out of there. At that moment Jack McVitie came out of the toilet and my mate pushed him into Reggie's way and made a dash for it.

He got clean away, owing his life to Jack 'the Hat' McVitie.

CHAPTER 12
BILLY FROST'S STORY

'If there ever was any trouble, we were well equipped to deal with it. We had gradually got together a real arsenal of weapons which we kept in various places.'
MY STORY, BY RONNIE KRAY

Let's talk guns.

Let's talk about a good friend of mine who used to hide weapons for the Twins. Let's talk about Billy 'Jack' Frost, as he was then known.

Billy learnt about weapons while in the army. He spent a lot of time shooting at Bisley and knew how to handle a weapon. Billy Frost and Billy Exley were the first two trusted members of the Kray Firm. They were loyal to the Twins and were liked by the East End people. Frostie, like Exley, was no liberty taker, unlike some on the Firm. Sadly Billy Exley has passed away but Billy Frost is still very much alive – and not a missing person, as John Pearson says in *The Profession Of Violence*. In fact, Billy still lives in the East End.

Frostie, as he is known, has done his spells in borstal and, in the 1950s, he was sentenced to five years' imprisonment and sent to Wandsworth. It was while in prison that Billy met his old friend Frank Mitchell. After a short stay in Wandsworth, Billy and Mitchell were sent to Dartmoor. Billy could see the end in sight but poor Frank couldn't.

While Billy was in Dartmoor he made friends with Roy Shaw, Eric Mason, Jimmy Essex and Mad Frankie Fraser. When Frostie was released from Dartmoor the Twins sent a Rolls-Royce to pick him up and bring him home. They gave him a coming out party, too, to welcome him back on the Firm.

Any time I saw Billy out or in a pub I would never hear him mention the Kray name. In fact, no one did. He was trusted without exception.

Frostie has been referred to as the 'Kray armourer', because he knew about firearms, but it was 'Split' Waterman that got hold of the guns for the Twins. Frostie simply hid some weapons for the Twins. Frostie used to take the guns from Waterman and wrap them in plastic bags and hid them in his mum's coal scuttle. However, this wasn't the best place to keep the firearms. Whenever the coal was shovelled about in there the bags that the guns were in would split and the firearms would get mucky. This was the reason why so many of the Kray guns would not fire or got jammed. Whether by accident or design, Frostie's hiding place saved a few people's lives.

Frostie went missing – just like Mad Teddy Smith. In fact, because Frostie disappeared at the same time as Smith many people believed he had been bumped off, too. That is why John Pearson had listed Frostie as missing in his book. The police listed him as missing as well. However, as Nipper Read admits in his book, Connie Whitehead had already spoken out about the disappearance of Frostie, but Read didn't see any mileage in trying to track him down. To this day Frostie is grateful for what Connie said. Frostie says that Connie should have never gone down with the Krays. He didn't do anything wrong and didn't like violence either, not the way the Twins conducted their violence.

Because Billy was a confidant of the Krays, he knew the way their minds worked. He tried to save Jack McVitie when he threatened to kill them. Billy told Jack to 'wipe his mouth and say no more', but Jack didn't and it wasn't long before he was being stabbed to death at Blonde Carol's.

Billy is a very good friend of mine, and the following is a story in his words about Ronnie Kray and his lust for firearms. The story takes place at the point when Charlie Kray made it clear to Frostie just how dangerous Ronnie was:

There is a story about Ronnie wanting to use two guns on one victim [Hugh McGowan] at the same time. Each gun to do a different job. 'I'm going to have a big gun and a little gun,' Ronnie said. 'I'm going to shoot McGowan first with the little gun, then I'm going to tell him all about it, then I'm going to shoot him right in the fucking head with the big gun [39]. He said this right in front of me and Charlie Kray. He said: 'You can be there Charlie and you can have a gun.' Then he turned to me and said: 'You can be there an' all.' And then he went out to do a pee. When he went out I laughed. Charlie said to me: 'Look, don't fuckin' laugh, *don't laugh*. I've got a wife and two kids. He fuckin' means it and I don't want to get

GETTING AWAY WITH MURDER

involved in murders.' You know Charlie was a family man, so he said to me: 'He really, really means it Billy.' The next day, I went around to the Twins' house and Ronnie said to me: 'I want you to do a little job today. I want you to take Stevie Till with you.' He gave me some money, 'Here,' he said, 'here's a fifty. I want you to go round the club and see if McGowan comes round there.' So me and Till went round there while Ronnie went somewhere else. When we got there McGowan wasn't there. I said, 'I'm not waiting here all day,' so after a while we went back. Ronnie said: 'Well, he should have been there because I've got some good information here.' And with that he forgot about it for a while.

Everybody knew Ronnie Kray was unstable and members of the Firm dealt with him in their own way. Most of them never really wanted to be part of a murder case, but sometimes it was unavoidable. You could not be close to the Krays and avoid murder. As Billy says of another Kray victim: 'They killed Ginger Frances. He was a grass. He wasn't on the Firm and I think he did a lot of damage to Foreman's Firm at some time. Harry Abraham's didn't like him either and gave him a hiding once. But when Ginger caused a lot of damage to the Kray Firm the Twins got rid of him.'

CHAPTER 13

BRIAN SCULLY

'I was born to be violent.'

REGGIE KRAY, IN *OUR STORY*, BY *RONNIE AND REGGIE KRAY*

Once upon a time, when Ronnie Kray killed George Cornell, he allegedly said to Reggie: 'I've done mine, now you do yours.'

Well I'm sorry to say that this is all lies. By the time Ronnie Kray killed George Cornell Reggie had already killed a man. This is his story.

It was while I was serving my time in 1956 in East Church Open Prison on the Isle of Sheppey in Kent that I made friends with two of the nicest men that I have ever met: Roy Wild and Brian Scully. Roy and Brian came from Hoxton and were already very good friends before they went into prison.

I kept up with Roy and Brian after we all got out and one

night we went to the Bacchus in Hoxton Market for a drink before we made our way up West to the Merry Go Round Club. Reggie and Ronnie came in with three or four of their Firm. The Krays stood at one end of the bar talking to the owner, while we were at the other end of the counter having a quiet drink.

As soon as I saw the Twins I felt uneasy, so I said to Roy and Brian that we should go somewhere else. They agreed, but Brian wanted to use the toilet before we left. He went in and a couple of minutes later we heard loud cries coming from the toilet. Just then, Reggie Kray came out of the toilet with his shirt and suit covered in blood. He got his boys together and they quickly left.

Roy and I ran into the toilet to find Brian sprawled on the floor covered in blood. Another man was also knocked out. While Roy was seeing to Brian, a couple of other blokes came in and helped me get the other man to his feet. We then carried Brian outside and put him in our car, taking him to hospital in Kingsland High Road.

When we got there Roy ran inside to get help. Once he had arranged for Brian to be safely taken inside we were told to go and sit in the waiting room. It seemed like hours just sitting there but it was only about ten minutes before the doctor came in and asked us what had happened to Brian. Roy gave him some cock and bull story. I don't know if the doctor believed it but he told us that Brian would have to have a few stitches and that they'd had to sedate him.

They decided to keep Brian in, so we left. When we were outside I asked Roy if he knew why Reggie had cut Brian. Roy told me that Brian had a bit of trouble with a girl some time back and when Brian had finished with her she went out with Reggie a few times. She then did a bit of mixing and Reggie decided to take it out on Brian.

I never saw Brian again because I was so busy travelling all over the country robbing country mansions and blowing a peter here and there ('peter' being a safe). I was also going on holiday a lot. It was only after this, while I was doing another term in prison, that I heard that Brian had been murdered by Reggie Kray. I really couldn't believe it. Brian wasn't a violent man. Far from it.

Later, while I was on the Kray case, I met up with Roy again when the police had found me a flat in Finchley. Roy moved in for a while. He told me what had happened. Brian had opened a workshop in Columbia Road, Bethnal Green, repairing three-piece suites. One day he was found with his throat cut. Roy told me that it had gone around the East End that Reggie was responsible for Brian's death. It was said that Brian slagged off Reggie a couple of times after he came out of hospital.

The police couldn't find out who had actually killed Brian. A wall of silence went up, built by the terrible fear that the Krays were capable of generating. But everyone in the East End knew what had happened, especially in the criminal fraternity. Reggie Kray wasn't satisfied with giving that poor man a beating, he had to go and finish the job. With what I know of the two Kray lunatics nobody can make me believe otherwise. The truth is that I have found this chapter very hard to write. Every time I discuss this episode tears come to my eyes. Brian was a lovely bloke and he really didn't deserve what Reggie Kray did to him. But then again, most of the

Kray victims didn't deserve the extreme measures inflicted upon them.

It was all senseless violence. As Connie Whitehead has said on television, you couldn't go out for a quiet drink without someone being hurt. I agree. As I've just related to you, that is exactly what happened to Brian. Not only that, but Reggie Kray then went back and hurt my dear old friend permanently. No one else was responsible. Brian didn't have enemies like that. It was Reggie Kray that did it.

CHAPTER 14
TONY MAFIA

'The world can only be ruled by fear.'
ADOLF HITLER

In his book *The Kray Brothers – The Image Shattered*, Craig Cabell revealed: 'Lambrianou claimed that two murders – possibly two of the murders investigated by Nipper Read... were Tony Mafia (aka the 'Magpie') and 'Scotch' Jack Buggy. Tony Mafia was found behind the wheel of his car, a bullet hole in the back of his head, while Buggy was allegedly pulled out of the sea at Brighton having been weighed down with lumps of rock and iron!'

The trouble with the Kray twins is that their violence really got out of hand. It reached a point where they thought that no matter what they did to people no one would dare go against them.

Charlie Kray was the one I felt sorry for in all of this, because he was a very nice man; a family man. I have been in the Krays' house when they have been slagging their elder brother off. Yes, it's true that Charlie was a fence for stolen property, like a lot of other people, but I can honestly say that I never saw Charlie behave violently to anyone. He was the exact opposite of the Twins and everyone in the East End respected him. That is why the Twins were jealous of him: Charlie got the respect; the Twins were hated. The Twins wanted all the attention, especially Ronnie. He couldn't get over the fact that Charlie was so well liked.

All Charlie wanted to be was a businessman, not a gangster. But because of those two horrible bastards his life was ruined. If they could do what they did to their own brother it clearly shows what lengths they would go to with non-family members.

Violence became a casual thing with Ronnie and Reggie, which leads me nicely into the story of Tony Mafia and Bullar Ward. Tony Lambrianou has gone on record as saying that Mafia was murdered by the Krays. That is not true, as I will explain in a moment. The following story doesn't just relate the truth about the death of Tony Mafia, it also shows the casual love affair with violence that the Krays enjoyed.

One night, Reggie Kray was drinking and taking pills in the Grave Maurice pub, when he decided to go to the Regency Club. When he walked into the club he saw Bullar Ward and Tony Mafia drinking at the bar.

Reggie walked up to Tony Mafia and started to demand money from him. To give credit to Bullar Ward he told Reggie to 'leave it out', that he was with Tony and that all they wanted was a quiet drink. With that, Reggie hit Bullar on the jaw and Bullar's reaction was the fatal words: 'You'll have to do better than that, mate.' Reggie did just that. He took a knife out of his pocket and cut Bullar right down the side of his face. Reggie left quickly after that because he knew that Bullar could hold his own.

Reggie had demanded the money as it was bandied around in the East End's criminal circles that Tony Mafia had organised a robbery at the Co-op Bank in Stratford, breaking into the deed boxes and stealing thousands of pounds worth of jewellery and gold coins that belonged to other criminals who had it put in there for safe-keeping. I was told by somebody on the Kray Firm that they had money deposited in there at the time. This person went on to say that it was a right liberty what Reggie did to Bullar, because he was a friend of theirs. Once again this proves what mad bastards they were.

I knew that Mafia was a fence for stolen goods because I'd sold some items to him in the past and I'd always found him to be a very genuine man.

Anyway, the result of all these rumours and confrontations was that Tony Mafia was found dead in his car. He had been shot in the back of the head on the Southend arterial road. Word soon went around the East End that the Krays did it. But on this occasion the rumours were wrong. Mafia was murdered by James Jewell, a bank robber. Jewel had a large sum of money deposited in the Co-op Bank and that was why he killed Mafia. Jewell was tried and sentenced to life imprisonment for the killing.

Mafia had made the cardinal sin: he had robbed his own.

Another murder that had nothing to do with the Krays was the killing of Thomas 'Ginger' Marks, who was shot from a moving vehicle in Cheshire Street, next to the Carpenter's Arms (the first pub the Twins ever owned). Cheshire Street runs parallel to the railway line and was adjacent to the Twins' house in Vallance Road, no more than a minute or two's walk from their front door. Because of the proximity and the tie-in with the Carpenter's Arms, some people suspected the Twins of Ginger's murder, but they had nothing to do with it. According to the first edition of Charlie Kray's book, *Me And My Brothers*, they were safely tucked up in bed at the time. Well, you can believe that if you wish. Charlie was probably telling the truth as he saw it.

The important thing to get from this chapter is the fact that the Krays didn't kill everyone who died in mysterious circumstances in the East End. I certainly don't want to blame them for everything – quite the opposite. I want to separate the fact from the fiction and make sure the truth of the murders that they *did* commit is known.

CHAPTER 15
JIMMY ANDREWS' STORY

Jimmy Andrews originally came from South London. He was in Dartmoor Prison in the 1950s with a very good friend of mine. Jimmy was a very tough man who became good friends with George Cornell. In time he moved across the water to live in North London. He was a good thief and he had many friends and was well known in the criminal world.

Jimmy's trouble started when he was in a West End drinking club and had a row with a very good friend of Jack McVitie's. I will not use this person's real name. I will call him Bob.

After Bob and Jimmy finished slagging each other off, Bob went to the Twins to see if they could sort things out. As a result, Reggie got in touch with Jimmy to organise a meeting between him and Bob in the Regency Club to settle their differences and shake hands. When the day came, Reggie and Bob were in the Regency Club waiting for Jimmy to arrive and when he did he was not on his own. He was team-handed.

I must give Reggie Kray his due. He went to the

Regency Club with Bob with all good intentions to settle the dispute between the two of them, but as Bob stretched out his hand to Jimmy all he got in return was a smack in the face. With this done, Jimmy Andrews turned and left the club with his friends.

Reggie was furious. He couldn't let Jimmy get away with what he had done. A few nights later Reggie and Bob plotted against Andrews and followed him to the Bagatelle Club, which was in Cork Street in the West End. Reggie waited until Andrews got out of his car before he started shooting at him. Unfortunately, with Reggie being near-sighted all he managed to hit was a load of dustbins. Andrews had a lucky escape that night.

A few weeks later Bob was driving by in his van when he spotted Andrews' car parked outside the Regency Club. He immediately went home and collected his sawn-off shotgun. He knew Andrews would be leaving the Regency soon as it was getting late. Bob drove his van and parked it opposite the flats where Andrews lived. A little while later a drunk Andrews arrived home in a cab, having left his car at the Regency. When Bob saw the cab pull up and Jimmy Andrews get out he ran up behind his man and shot him in the leg. The blast almost blew Andrews' limb clean off.

Andrews managed to crawl to a neighbour's flat and bang on the door. The police and an ambulance were called and Andrews was taken to the London Hospital, where he was put into intensive care. What was left of his leg was amputated. What I admired about Jimmy Andrews is that when the police were finally able to question him about the shooting he told them not to worry as he would settle things himself.

Unfortunately, Jimmy Andrews never did get his revenge. He was struck down with terminal cancer and died in the London Hospital.

The thing to remember here is that a straightforward row between two men spiralled out of control once the Krays got involved and one of them ended up shot and almost mortally wounded. This is the sort of thing that happened when the Krays decided to intervene in other people's affairs.

CHAPTER 16

THE BANK MANAGER

This book concentrates on the Kray murders. But for it to also provide a complete picture of the deaths they perpetrated then one must look more closely at the frauds they committed as well.

The Kray twins weren't just murderers, they were also bullies. When you acknowledge that fact in connection to their extortions, protection rackets and long-firm frauds, you uncover another legacy of terror that affected people with a flair for finance.

There were many counts of fraud that Nipper Read wanted to charge the Kray twins with. But as the Twins had already been handed life sentences for murder, Read was not encouraged to follow up the frauds and financial crimes of the Krays. This denied the public the opportunity to discover the full range and extent of the Krays' activities – and to see to what lengths some people would go to escape their clutches, including committing suicide.

The only evidence we have of a suicide caused by

association with the Kray Firm came *after* the Twins had been imprisoned. Maybe some people did kill themselves because of their direct contact with the Twins but I don't have any proof of that, at least not yet. However, a bank manager was apparently driven to suicide because of the fraud perpetrated on him and his bank by certain former Kray Firm members and associates.

People fail to remember that the Twins ordered the execution of Leslie Payne, and that it was only by sheer luck that he avoided being gunned down by Ronnie and Reggie's henchmen. Payne knew all about the Twins' financial affairs – too much, as it turned out, which is why the brothers wanted him dead. Then look at the suicide of poor Frances Shea, forced to kill herself rather than endure another moment of life within the Kray family. It is clear that the Twins would do anything to protect what they saw as theirs, whether it was their money or their reputation. If anyone was beaten up, assaulted or died – whether by murder or suicide – then that was too bad.

I want to include a little pause for thought here. The Twins are accused of having a 'reign of terror' or 'demanding respect', but these phrases do not convey the depths of despair that their crimes sent people to. Some people, innocent people, were driven down so much by the Twins' lust for power and money that they committed the ultimate act of desperation: they took their own lives. And it was not just the Krays that made people do this; key members of their Firm drove people to suicide as well.

CHAPTER 17

THE ONES WE DON'T KNOW ABOUT

Nipper Read has explained that the Krays were almost certainly responsible for other murders and that he investigated some of them himself. Because of this, he knows more than most how difficult it is to gather any evidence at all about some of the lesser-known homicides. He has said: 'These were people who during the course of their exploits came up against the Krays and for one reason or another fell out with them. Anybody who stood in their way drew the short straw, but it was hard to get the evidence needed to convict them. Teddy Smith was known. He had plays on TV; but the other people who disappeared were small villains like Cornell or McVitie.'

Nipper Read spent two years with his trusty team researching the Krays' activities. He had feelers out everywhere. He admits that it was difficult to get people to come forward to give evidence about the murders, but eventually they did. If you rule with fear, people will fear you; and if people fear you, they will want to eventually escape your clutches. As the Krays grew more and more paranoid and began to threaten the lives of their own close associates and families, so those associates began to turn on the Twins.

In this situation, Read and his team were able to build up a wider picture of the Krays' criminal activities – and discover that there were many more murders than was originally suspected. I'm not sure if the extra murders that Nipper Read suspected correspond to the extra murders detailed here. In some ways it does not really matter. The point is that, in time, people came to realise that the Krays' crimes were much worse than originally suspected. This book details the old East Enders' story of the Krays, people like myself, Billy Frost and Eric Mason. We all knew the Krays and saw a lot of what happened.

Yes, there could be other murders. More murders even than the ones put down in this book and possibly others that were noted down in Nipper Read's files [40]. Ask other members of the former East End criminal underworld – former members of the Kray Firm – and they may come up with even more names.

Whatever the final total, it's still too many. And I tell you something else: there are people in the East End who wished they had never met the Kray twins. Youngsters open their eyes wide at the sound of their name, but some of us older people don't, because we know the bitter truth about them or, at least, know enough about them to look away and shake our heads in disgust.

If there are indeed other murders then my heart goes out to the victims' families. Nobody truly gets over the death of a loved one. There's always an empty place in the heart for them to reside and the Krays left many an empty space in this world.

The other side of the coin is that when you have a fearsome reputation anything can be heaped on you and you get blamed for all sorts of things. As the Krays are no longer here to account for themselves we should ensure that we are more than scrupulous when laying the blame for crimes at their door. One reason why I mention this is because a story came to light while I was writing this book that Lord Lucan was disposed of by the Krays. Madness, surely? But nevertheless the story has been put out there and some people may be prepared to believe it.

The stories related in this book have been rumoured for decades. It was only when a group of us got together and talked that the real truth came out. At no time was the Lord Lucan story ever mentioned. I really don't know where that came from and, frankly, it doesn't interest me or concern the thrust of this book. What is written down here many people in the East End would support. We know the Krays killed other people. We don't need sensational headline stories clutched out of thin air because the truth is stranger than fiction. In my world, one doesn't have to go far to hear true, first-hand stories concerning the Kray twins.

Seven murders or seventy, it's still far too many.

CHAPTER 18

BILLY BANNISTER

Many stories have been told about the Krays, but the truly valid tales are those told by the East Enders who were there and saw the Twins operate during their reign of terror.

I have seen with my own eyes hardened criminals cower down before them and I have seen the terror in some people's faces when Ronnie Kray was giving them a talking to. I had the same experience. I was forced to look into the cold eyes of Ronnie Kray as he branded me with pokers. I pissed myself. And he got sexual pleasure out of it. Ronnie Kray got sexual pleasure out of my terror.

My opinion of Ronnie Kray is that he was an abortion of nature, a freak. As for Reggie Kray? He was just as dangerous as his twin. He cut people up and he was a murderer. He, too, was a freak of nature.

I was in their Kentucky Club one night having a drink with a couple of mates when two young boys walked in. They were having a drink and enjoying themselves until one of the boys went to the toilet and I saw Ronnie follow him in. Within minutes you could hear the boy screaming, then Ronnie dragged the boy out and along the floor. He then threw him through a glass-panelled door. I don't know what went on in the toilet that night but I was told afterwards that Ronnie paid the boy's father a sum of money for him not to go to the police. That's another crime they got away with.

The Twins had bent police in their pockets, too. It was part of the reason why they thought they could do just as they pleased and get away with it. They honestly felt untouchable.

The Twins would hold their meetings with the Firm in the Widows pub on Tapp Street, or sometimes upstairs in their own house, where Mrs Kray would take tea and sandwiches up for them. The one thing I must give the Twins credit for was the fact that they would not cause trouble in front of their mother. If they ever had the needle with anyone on the Firm, they would settle their differences away from her home. This was a maxim that the Twins lived by. I'm not praising them for it; after all, it didn't stop them ruining peoples lives away from Vallance Road.

I remember once they got in touch with a good friend of mine, Billy Bannister, whom I got to know while I was doing time in Wandsworth. We had become inseparable. He was a very good thief in his day until he was grassed up by an old flame who was jealous of him living with another woman. For this nasty act of revenge Billy was given a four-year prison sentence.

I had not seen Billy Bannister for a couple of weeks when I was walking along Old Compton Street in Soho and bumped into him, so we went and had a drink in a pub opposite the Windmill Theatre. After we'd had a couple I could see that he had something on his mind, so I asked him if he was OK. I told him that if he had money problems I could let him have some to tide him over. He told me that he didn't have any money problems but that he did have a big problem with the Twins. He went on to say that they had stuck up a big jewel heist for him to pull off. They had told him that the payoff would be in the thousands.

I asked him what the problem was and he replied that he thought the Twins were setting him up as a favour to some of their bent coppers. I told him that they would never do anything like that because they loved money too much. I did not want to know anything about the job or when and where he was going to do it, but he told me anyway. He gave me the whole story. When he had finished I sat there in shock: the man they wanted Billy to rob was both a very good friend of mine and the Twins.

While Billy went to get another drink I sat there thinking what I was going to say to him when he got back. I have always stood by the code that you do not rob or hurt your own. It's a pity those two bastards didn't think the same way, so I said to Billy that if he did the job he would only get a small percentage of the takings. It would be better, I said, if he allowed himself to get caught doing a little job so that he would be sent away for a few months. That way he would have a watertight alibi not to do the job the Krays were setting up for him. I also told him that we had never had that conversation!

That was the last time I ever saw Billy. He didn't do the job and went away for about three months.

A little while after that I was in the company of a couple of men from the Kray Firm in the Regency Club. They told me that they had to get away from the Twins and I replied that the Twins would never let them go because they knew too much. I also told them that I had come out for a quiet drink and didn't want to talk about the Twins. However, they did and we ended up sitting at a little table in the corner where they told me of a fellow by the name of Billy who had crossed the Twins a couple of weeks previously. Apparently, the Twins had the duo drive them to a drinking club in North London where Billy was drinking with a friend of theirs. When they got there they waited in the car until people started coming out of the club. They waited nearly an hour for Billy to come out. When he did, he was drunk and could hardly stand. Ronnie said: 'That's the man.' They pulled the car up next to the drunk and the Twins got out and started cutting him up. When Billy fell to the floor, they picked him up and put him in the boot of the car.

The Twins got into the back of the car and told the Firm members to drive them home. When they got there Ronnie opened the boot and said: 'He won't cross us anymore, he's dead.'

I sat there in complete shock. I couldn't help feeling that it was all my fault. If I hadn't told Billy to go away for a while he would probably still be alive.

They never knew that Billy was my friend and his death has haunted me ever since. I would just like to say: Billy, wherever you are, I'm deeply sorry.

CHAPTER 19

ALAN BRUCE COOPER

Alan Bruce Cooper was born the son of Jewish parents in Chicago, USA. In the early 1920s his father, Joseph Cooper, was involved in organised crime with some of the country's most notorious bootlegging gangs. Sometimes he would drive for Lucky Luciano who, in those days, was one of the most powerful gangsters in America. Joseph was a colourful character. He walked with a pronounced limp, which he acquired breaking his ankle after jumping out of a whore house window during a police raid.

When WWII broke out Joseph's son Alan joined the American army. Towards the end of the War, when the Allies were making their way through Germany, Alan Cooper and some friends decided to rob a bank. Unfortunately for them, they were caught and court-martialled, which resulted with Alan receiving seven years in Fort Worth prison.

The first time I heard of Alan Bruce Cooper was on one of the many occasions that I frequented Joe Coral's Spieler in Stamford Hill, where I had made friends with a very nice

Jewish man who turned out to be Alan's father, Joseph. As my friendship with Joseph grew I would sit with him over a glass of lemon tea and I would be fascinated with the stories he told me about the time he lived in Chicago. I often wondered what had made him and his family come to live in the East End. He never told me why. I never asked him because I thought it was none of my business. Anyway, all this is preparatory to the fact that I would one day become his son's chauffeur.

During the mid-1960s Alan Bruce Cooper lived in Camden Hill Court in Holland Park with his wife Beverley and their daughter. He got involved with the Twins during the course of one of his shady deals. Little did they know that Alan Bruce Cooper had been planted in their Firm to help the police gather as much information about the Krays as they could. Reggie and Charlie were suspicious of Cooper, but Ronnie got his own way.

It was Ronnie Kray's lifelong ambition to go to America and meet some Mafia figures. When Ronnie told Reggie and Charlie they declined to go along and even tried to talk Ronnie out of going himself. But Ronnie would not be swayed. His brothers stayed at home and he took Dickie Morgan with him instead.

Everything was arranged. The flights were booked and they were first to fly to France and visit the American Embassy to collect the necessary paperwork that would allow them into the country. Ronnie and Dickie's prison records in the UK meant that they were unable to get the correct documents at home. When Ronnie and Dickie arrived in France, they were taken straight to the American Embassy. Once there, they were told to sit down while their papers were arranged. With their connections, everything was sorted out.

In America Ronnie Kray was wined and dined and treated like the British royalty that he probably thought he was. When he got home he couldn't wait to tell Reggie and Charlie about his experiences in the States. This was a great time for the Twins. They truly felt invincible. But as they played gangsters and nightclub hosts to celebrities they failed to notice that someone had begun to take a very keen interest in their life of crime – Nipper Read.

Read and his crack squad of investigators were based in Tintagel House, on the southern embankment of the Thames. They deliberately based themselves away from Scotland Yard as Read felt that he could not trust some of the officers based there who may have had Kray connections. Read was only accountable to one man for the Kray case, John Durose, who gave him a lot of flexibility because he wanted the Krays behind bars as much as Read.

Read knew that it was going to be a hard fight for him and his team, but throughout his investigations one name kept cropping up: Alan Bruce Cooper. Read went to see Cooper and was surprised to find that Cooper was already working directly for Durose. He was effectively a double agent. Reggie and Charlie Kray had been right not to trust him all along.

Alan Bruce Cooper was a small man who spoke with a stutter. Like his father, he walked with a limp. But he was good with words and, like Leslie Payne, could talk the hind legs off a donkey.

When the Kray case was over and the brothers and Firm members were all locked up in prison, I was dropped from the Police Protection Scheme. I was living in Finchley at the time and at a loose end. I had no job and, with my prison record, little chance of finding one. Then I saw an ad in a newspaper one day which stated that a Mr Henry Ronson of Hampstead was looking for a chauffeur with Rolls-Royce experience. I called him up and explained that I had passed the Rolls-Royce School of Driving exam and had my certificate to prove it.

I was invited to his house for an interview and after giving him some old cock and bull story I was taken on as his personal chauffeur. He was a nice man and I got on well with him, but the job was not to last.

I was out of work again so I got in touch with a good friend of mine who offered me a little job, which I did. I received a few thousand for that, which allowed me to live in style for a while. It at least allowed me to pay my rent and have a few drinks in my favourite pub, the Princess of Prussia in Finchley Central. Trouble was, I missed the East End.

One day I was walking along Ballards Lane and a big green Mercedes pulled up alongside me. Inside was Ivor Bloom. We went and had a few drinks and he asked me what I was getting up to. I told him that I was getting fed up with doing nothing and being away from the East End and everyone I knew. That was when he told me that Alan Cooper was looking for a driver who he could trust to look after his Rolls-Royce. Like me, Cooper had been a major witness in the Kray case, so who better than me to go and work for him?

The following day I went with Ivor Bloom to meet Alan

Cooper in his flat in Marble Arch. It was an impressive place, with a security guard in the building foyer. When Ivor rang the flat's doorbell, a maid answered and showed us into a very lavishly furnished room. That was when I was first introduced to Alan Bruce Cooper and his beautiful wife, Beverley. We were then joined by a small, slim lady whose husband, it turned out, was in prison and serving out a sentence because of Cooper.

I had made up my mind to go when the maid came in with a tray of drinks. I was left alone with Cooper and we had a long conversation about the Twins and then what my duties would be if I became his driver. I began to warm to Cooper as we talked but I still thought that he was a man you had to be wary of. After we had finished our conversation he offered me the job and a generous salary. I said yes and we shook hands on it. I was now Alan Bruce Cooper's driver.

That afternoon I took him for a spin round the West End in his Rolls. We ended up outside a posh-looking shop in Newman Street called Garret Fine Arts. Cooper told me that he owned the shop – and that when I wasn't driving him around it would be my job to look after the shop as a kind of manager.

I had been working for Cooper for about two months and I had left Finchley by this time and Cooper had found me a lovely flat in Colindale, which he paid the rent on.

Leslie Payne walked into the shop one day. He had given evidence for the prosecution in the trial of the Krays. Another two right old slags came in. One of them was the man that the Richardsons had supposedly tortured. The other man was a slimy bastard who was into all sorts of criminal activities.

Payne offered me his hand but I declined to shake it. Cooper was there and said that he didn't know that Leslie and I knew each other. With a crafty smirk Payne said: 'Of course I know Lenny, he's one of the old school.'

Just then another man came into the shop carrying some fine-looking oil paintings by famous artists. As I stood there listening to Payne prattle on my blood began to boil. I had to get out of there, so I told Cooper that I was going to get something to eat. I, for one, didn't want anything to do with the likes of Payne and his cronies. After Payne and his entourage eventually left the shop I handed Cooper the keys to his Rolls-Royce and told him to get another driver.

But Cooper talked me into staying, and from that day on one of my main jobs was to drive him and his associates to a number of banks around London. Cooper would hand me £200 at the end of each day. He even bought me a car as a present for being so loyal to him. The last bank I ever drove Cooper to was the Barclays Bank in Bexleyheath, Kent. For the next few weeks after we'd been to the bank Cooper didn't seem himself. His so-called friends and associates stopped coming around as well, so I could tell that something was up.

Then, one day, I took him to meet a man who I knew to be one of the police officers from the Kray case. When Cooper came back to the car he was as white as a sheet and looked very worried. He told me to take him to the American embassy, and from there we went on to the Hilton Hotel in Park Lane. Cooper told me to go back to his flat and tell his wife to pack him a suitcase: he had to leave the country. Fast. He would be staying in a hotel that night, in the suite of an arms-dealer friend of his, but after that he was off.

I went to see Cooper's wife and she handed me a holdall that contained thousands of pounds to give to her husband. When I got back to the hotel I asked Cooper what was going on. He knew he could trust me, so he told me that the man he met with earlier that day had told him that the police were coming round to his flat at 6:00 a.m. the next morning to arrest him for fraud. He told me that he had been swindling the banks that I had been driving him to.

I left Cooper at his hotel that night and came back the next morning at 5:00 a.m. to take him to Rochford Airport, near Southend. On the way there Cooper told me that he could arrange for me to go and live with him in Phoenix, Arizona. Once we got to the airport we said our goodbyes – and that was the last I ever saw of Alan Bruce Cooper. Some time later, I read in one of the national newspapers that the manager of the Barclays Bank in Bexleyheath had hung himself (see Chapter 16). I had to wonder if it had been because of Cooper and his associates. It turned out that Reggie and Charlie were right not to trust Cooper. He had his fingers in so many pies that it was unbelievable.

With Cooper gone, I then went to work as a driver in France for a man called Bob Gould. We travelled all over, through the Pyrenees and into Andorra, and then on to Madrid. Bob Gould finally retired and went to live in Portugal, where he bought a large house. If he's still alive today I wish him all the very best.

CHAPTER 20

BILLY EXLEY AND THE KRAYS' DOWNFALL

'Let me put in your minds, if yours forget / What you have been ere now, and what you are / Withal, what I have been, and what I am.'

RICHARD III, BY WILLIAM SHAKESPEARE

E ric Mason, Billy Frost and Billy Exley were the three men that the Twins knew they could rely upon and trust above all others. This really meant something, as the Krays usually kept a lot to themselves. This is why it is so difficult (as it was for Nipper Read) to piece their life of crime together.

In the early 1960s the Twins both began to drink heavily, following in the footsteps of their father. They were also taking drugs, especially Ronnie, who was on medication to ease his schizophrenia. This made the Twins even more unstable than they already were. As well as hurting people outside the Firm they also began to hurt people inside it: Connie Whitehead, who was one of Ronnie Kray's drivers in the early 1960s, was about to be killed by Ronnie until other members of the Firm talked him out of it. Connie, as I knew him, was very loyal to the Krays, so there you have an example of how they repaid the respect shown to them.

As if all this wasn't bad enough, the Twins then turned against Billy Exley, one of their most trusted men. Ronnie was particularly paranoid at the time and in his mad-sick mind he decided that he was going to kill Billy Exley at any cost.

Exley had earned the Twins' displeasure after a con that they set up went wrong. They knew that they were being watched by Scotland Yard detectives and they needed money in order to leave the country. To get it, they hatched a plan with Exley to con two businessmen out of a lot of money. The meet took place in the Widows pub and before the two businessmen arrived the Twins went over their final plans to make sure that Exley knew what he had to say. The two businessmen arrived, the money the Krays wanted in their briefcase, and the meeting got underway. The Twins began to spin their story and things went well for a while, with the businessmen looking convinced. That is, until it was Exley's turn to speak. To Ronnie Kray's astonishment, Exley forgot his lines and leaned across the table and asked: 'What do I say?' The two businessmen immediately became suspicious. They quickly said their goodbyes, took their money and left.

Ronnie Kray went into one of his many rages. He tipped over the table, yelling the most vile abuse imaginable at Exley. The Twins were desperate for that money and it's a wonder that Ronnie didn't kill Exley there and then. Fortunately for Billy, Charlie Kray was at the bar and he managed to calm Ronnie down. He told Ronnie that Exley was a little gullible and he should have used somebody else. Ronnie told Exley: 'You'll pay for this, you'll get no pension money for a couple of months.' This meant that Exley would lose the £10 per week that was given to him by the Krays.

This loss of income affected Billy Exley because he had a wife and family. To make some money he got himself involved with some Turkish-Cypriot terrorists in North London. He was making a good living with them until the Krays found out about it and put the word out that they wanted to see him at Vallance Road right away.

Exley turned up at Fort Vallance a couple of days later, wondering what he could have done to upset the Twins. He knew that he was in no immediate danger because the Krays would never inflict any violence on someone under their own mother's roof. When Exley arrived at Vallance Road he was shown into the living room, where Ronnie and Reggie were waiting for him, along with Charlie Kray and Billy Frost. No sooner had Exley entered the Kray living room than Ronnie went into one, calling Exley all the names under the sun. Charlie and Billy Frost finally got Ronnie to calm down, but not before he'd told Exley: 'If you weren't in my mother's house you would be fucking dead.'

Exley asked what he was meant to have done. 'I'll tell you what you are doing that is fucking wrong you silly bastard,' Ronnie fumed. 'Don't you know that those fucking terrorists you are hanging about with in North London have got MI5 watching them? And we have got all of fucking Scotland Yard watching us. Don't you think we have got enough on our plate without you bringing us more fucking grief?' After all the shouting and hollering was done, Ronnie Kray told Exley to fuck off, adding that he was a 'dead man walking', because he had ruined Ronnie and Reggie's chance to leave the country. Then Ronnie Kray threatened to kill Exley's wife and family.

This was one of the biggest mistakes that Ronnie Kray ever made. Exley had been a true friend to the Twins over the years – and he knew that when Ronnie made a threat it was always carried out, one way or the other. To protect his family, Exley went to Nipper Read. In return for police protection he told Read what he knew, eventually ending up giving evidence in the Mitchell trial.

I for one am glad that Billy Exley had the guts to give evidence against the Krays, something I know he would never have done in a million years if Ronnie hadn't threatened his family. I know what Exley went through because I had been put in the same position myself. Billy Exley was always a very dear friend to me and now he has passed on from this world of ours and out of the Krays' clutches I want you to know that he will always be sadly missed by me and his dear old pal Billy Frost. God bless you Billy.

The police did finally round up the Turkish–Cypriot terrorists and had them thrown out of the country. By that time both the Krays had become paranoid, believing that they could trust no one. They had Firm members watching each other and reporting back to them if it was thought somebody was informing the police or getting up to anything behind their backs. By that time Ronnie Kray's paranoid schizophrenia had taken full control of him and he was beginning to hallucinate. Some of the Firm realised that Ronnie was stark staring mad and began to make themselves scarce, staying away from their usual haunts. This really got up the Twins' noses, especially as their elder brother Charlie also began to see as little of them as possible. I know this because Charlie was my friend and I know that his patience was running out with his brothers.

And then it came to pass. After two years of patiently gathering together information on the Krays, Nipper Read arrested the Twins and their associates. It was the end of the Firm. Once arrested, Ronnie and Reggie knew that they never had a chance of getting away with any of their notorious crimes. So Nipper Read gave them a choice: if they held up their hands to all three murders he would let the Firm go free. But they were having none of that and took most of the Firm down with them – apart from those who had turned Queen's Evidence. Nipper and his team's job was done. They had worked hard and it had paid off. The Twins were behind bars, where they belonged.

Even today people still get misty-eyed about the Krays, saying that if they were still around there would be no muggings or street crime. Older folks also say that the Twins were good to them because they would put their hands in their pockets and give them a pound note or two. What they don't ask themselves is where that money came from: innocent people, that's where. The only reason they did a bit of charity work was to give people a false impression of themselves and, in some cases, it worked. But those of us who lived in the criminal world knew exactly where the Twins were coming from and they could not pull the wool over our eyes. There is only one person that you can blame for the Krays' downfall and that is Ronnie Kray. He was truly mad and if he had not been put away there's no telling how many more people would have suffered at his hands. He had a fascination with seeing people in pain and I pray to God that we will never see the likes of the Kray twins again. They were this country's first two queer celebrity gangsters and, I hope, the last. Judge Melford Stevenson got it right when he said that we deserved a long rest from the Twins, sending them down with a recommendation that they serve *at least* 30 years each in prison. And now, after spending half their lives inside, they are both dead.

What a waste.

CHAPTER 21

MEN I HAVE KNOWN

The Morgans were a good family who lived in Mile End. I have known them for more than 60 years. I went to school with the eldest brother, who was known to everyone round the East End as Chunky Morgan because of his size.

Dickie was the second eldest. I knew him from when he and the Levy family used to hang about the Mile End streets. There was also a younger Morgan brother. Dickie Morgan was friendly with the Twins and when they got conscripted into the army, Dickie was sent to the Tower of London with them. Dickie and the Twins decided that army life was not for them. They could not take orders from anyone. One morning, when they had to stand by their beds for a kit inspection, the officer who was carrying out the inspection shouted at Reggie. In response, Reggie punched him on the chin and knocked him out. Ronnie decided to get a piece of the action and started to give the officer a kicking. When the Twins were finished, along with Dickie, they walked out the gates and went AWOL.

When all three were finally caught they were sent to Shepton Mallet. On their release they were given a court martial and thrown out of the army with dishonourable discharges. Dickie Morgan was by now more like a brother to the Krays. He stayed very loyal to the them the whole time that he was with then. That is until the Twins were arrested.

When Nipper Read and Mr Cater burst into Ronnie and Reggie's mother's flat in Braithwaite House to arrest the Twins, they found Reggie in bed with a young girl and Ronnie in bed with a young boy.

The Twins called some of their once loyal friends 'traitors' once they went down. In my opinion, they were the biggest traitors of them all because they would not own up to the murders they had committed, thus taking their associates down with them.

As for Dickie Morgan, he was fun to be with. He wasn't a violent man, although he could look after himself. The Krays broke the East End code over and over again because they hurt and robbed their own – and when the going got tough all they could think about was themselves.

So there is Dickie Morgan. Not a gangster, just a young man in the Kray story who hung about with them, shared some good times and then was let down. He was a man I knew and liked. To you, he's probably just another Kray gang member? But he wasn't. He was a regular bloke from the East End. Please remember the difference.

I couldn't write this book without writing a bit about my great friend Harry Abrahams. Harry was born in the East End. He lived with his mother, father and two younger brothers. His father was of Jewish descent and his mother was born in Swansea, Wales.

Harry's dad, Joe Abrahams, was an ex-professional boxer and an army champion. Harry took up boxing in his early teens and he became a very good amateur, winning all his fights. He won most of them by knockout. In those days, in the early 1950s, every area had its own gangs. For example, you had the Islington Gang, the Bethnal Green Gang, the Stepney and Watney Street Gangs, and also the Poplar, Canning Town and Manor Park Gangs. The most lethal outfit was the up-and-coming Bethnal Green Gang. And yes, the Twins led that one.

It was in those early days that Harry joined up with the Krays and went on the Firm. The Twins liked Harry because he was smart and could handle himself. He was afraid of no one.

Harry stayed with the Twins until the late 1950s, when he'd finally had enough of the direction they were going. He then set up his own gang. Unlike the Krays', Harry's gang was made up of very good thieves. Once Harry got his gang organised they got their money doing blags (robbing security vans). Harry started making a lot of money, but as fast as the money was made it was gone. So they would go out and do another blag. This went on until the decision was made to rob banks.

I met Harry and joined his gang around 1960, but all I was there for was to be Harry's personal driver. Harry had a lovely wife by the name of Jean. They had two daughters. In time, Jean became one of the best friends I ever had until she sadly passed away some years ago.

Jean divorced Harry when she found out that he'd been

going to all-night parties with Albert Donoghue and a couple of gang members and was using prostitutes. Funnily enough, the girl that Harry used was also called Jean. She was very good looking; she was also a very nice girl.

One Saturday night I went along to one of these parties. It wasn't really my scene. Everyone was drinking dark rum and coke in those days. I was not much of a drinker then, so I stuck to brown ale. Records were blaring out, songs by Chubby Checker, 'The Twist' and 'Humpty Dumpty'. People were starting to get drunk, and I found myself sitting on the settee talking to an Irish girl whose husband happened to be in prison. Then I looked up and saw this gorgeous blonde girl.

When the music stopped, one of Harry's mates came over to me and said: 'Len, see that blonde girl I was dancing with? She fancies you.' To tell you the truth, I did not believe him. He told me that a slow record was being put on because she wanted to dance with me. When the record came on she made her way over to me. I got up and we danced. I kept thinking to myself that the whole thing was a set-up, but I carried on with it. It was while we were dancing that she said she was tired and would I be so kind as to drive her home in her sports car. I told Harry and he said: 'You lucky bastard, go and enjoy yourself.' When the girl had said her goodbyes, we got in her sports car and I drove her home to a plush set of flats in Kensington. I parked her car in the garage and she kissed me as we got out. She had on a very short mini skirt and the most beautiful pair of legs I have ever seen – with a figure to match!

When we got into her flat my breath was taken away. Her

flat was one of the most beautiful apartments that I had ever seen. It was spotless and the bar was made up of different coloured glass. She threw her coat onto a chair and she said: 'Lets have a drink.' She made some lovely cocktails and kissed me a couple of times. I remember thinking: What have I got that makes her fancy me? I couldn't believe my luck. After a few more drinks she asked me if I would like to stay the night with her. I told her without hesitation that I would love to. With that, she told me to help myself to a drink while she changed into something casual.

While she was gone I kept saying to myself: Am I dreaming? I poured myself another drink, and it was then that she suddenly appeared in a lace negligée. However, the blonde wig was now gone. She had a DA haircut. She was a gay fella in drag!

I couldn't get out of there quick enough. I still had the keys to her car, which I drove back to the party. When I rang the doorbell the curtains moved and everyone looked out and started laughing. Harry opened the door and said to me: 'Come in, love. We've a lovely redhead inside who's dying to meet you.'

I told him to fuck off.

I was a little naïve about the workings of the West End, so I had to put it all down to experience. It wasn't long after this that Harry's wife found out about the parties and threw him out. Harry soon met another lovely girl named Dennise and they had a son together.

Around 1963 Harry and his gang did a bank in Hackney. It was a cold and rainy day. Harry was outside in the getaway car and all the car windows were closed and steamed up so nobody could see in. Even so, Harry was picked out on an identity parade. We all knew that Harry had been grassed up. He went to the Old Bailey and got five years. When he came out he went straight into a job for a gown manufacturing company.

There was a lot of unhappiness in Harry's life. His first wife Jean died and his two brothers committed suicide. When his father died, Harry started drinking heavily while living with his lovely mother, Renee. Harry died a few years ago now. Before he passed away I went to see him in the Royal Free Hospital in Hampstead and I hardly recognised him. He was a shell of his former self. His mother died not long after him. As for Jean the prostitute, she married a nice Jewish boy and moved out of London. I don't know if she or her husband are still alive, but I do know that I lost one of my best friends in Harry Abrahams. God bless you Harry, you will always be in my heart.

There's one more person I want to tell you about: David Levy.

David came from a large Jewish family and I was on very good terms with them all. Artie Levy was one of my best mates.

The Levys lived in Maidman Street off Burdett Road. They were well respected in the area and would take no nonsense from anybody. David Levy was the fighter in the family. He would not bow down to anyone. Even the local tearaways were very wary of him because he was the local governor of the area. Even so, David was one of the nicest men you could meet. He was always very polite. He could not stand a bully and he had no time for flash people.

His sister Betty married a man called Freddy Bird, who for some reason had fallen out with Reggie Kray. David Levy was visiting his sister one day when a car pulled up outside her house and Reggie Kray got out and barged past David into the house. His intention was to hurt Freddy – that is, until David jumped between them. Reggie pulled a knife, so David picked up a bread knife and stabbed Reggie in the guts. Reggie left with his tail firmly between his legs. There was no comeback from Reggie Kray on David and from that day forward Reggie and David became very good friends.

The last time I saw David was when we were both in prison. I was working on an outside party making tea for the other cons. My job was to collect the tea urns and sandwiches from the cookhouse where David worked as a cook. David said that he would cook me a large lump of bacon and told me where he would hide it for me to pick up. In return, I told him that I had hidden some drink and tobacco outside, which I brought back in with me that evening for him.

When I got back to the prison I found this nicely wrapped portion of lovely, cooked bacon, which I put down my trousers. I walked back to my cell with my hands in my pockets, holding onto the bacon. Suddenly, somebody shouted behind me: 'Take your hands out of your fucking pockets you little bastard.' At first I thought that it was one of the other cons trying to frighten me, but when I turned around I saw to my amazement that it was the prison governor and the chief. As soon as I took my hands out of my pockets the bacon slipped down my trouser leg and fell to the floor. I was banged up in chokey overnight and sent to see the governor the next morning. He gave me 14 days of bread and water and I lost one month of remission on top.

The whole point of this chapter is to acknowledge the larger-than-life characters that didn't go around slashing and killing people in the East End. It's also to highlight the heavy price that being a criminal brings.

I have been halfway round the world and I've met some very nice people along the way. I now have a beautiful partner, Gwen, and a gorgeous daughter, Katie. If I had my life again, I wouldn't change a thing. What I will say to all the younger readers of this book is: Don't go down the wrong path; life is too short and you must realise that no one lives forever. I hope you take heed and listen to the words of an old fool. Trust me for what I am saying to you. I don't know how many times I have heard people say that if they could only turn the clock back their lives would be different. I have said these words myself. As the saying goes, the day you are born that's the day you start dying. And remember, king of the underworld or ordinary Joe, we all go to our grave in a pine box. Just enjoy yourselves and don't look for glamour in crime. It doesn't exist. I believe it was Shakespeare who said: 'Bind your friends to your heart with hoops of steel.' Don't go behind bars.

CHAPTER 22

AND NOTHING BUT THE TRUTH...

'Holmes rose and sat down at the table with his pen
in his hand and a bundle of paper before him.
"Just tell us the truth," he said. "I shall jot down the facts.
You will sign it, and Watson here can witness it",'
The Boscombe Valley Mystery,
by Sir Arthur Conan Doyle

Before I conclude this book and present some additional interviews, notes and records to back up my memories, I want to take a moment to reflect upon the people who have put me down or spoken lies about the Twins and the Firm.

Some may think that I've already had my say in that department, but here it is again, so take heed. I was there, my friends were there and this is our story – the true story of how the Krays got away with murder. There is no agenda here, unlike in so many other books by people who claim to know it all.

In short, my sole purpose in writing my story about the Krays is because I'm fed up reading comments by people who didn't come from the East End and who never met the Twins and their associates. To be honest, and I mean this with all sincerity, I would never have been a witness against the Krays if they had not threatened to kill my two children.

So much has been said about the Twins, some of it true and a lot of it lies. The real truth is that they brought about their own downfall by cutting and carving up people in the East End. Then they went to the extreme of killing people. Only people who were in the East End in those days knew what it was like to live through the Krays' reign of terror. I have been on many different television programmes to voice my honest opinion about the Twins, and people that lived in the East End know everything that I have said in this book is the truth.

And yet the Kray legend continues. For example, I did not go on national television to slag the Krays off, as one Kray apologist, Steve Wraith, has said. Wraith lives in Newcastle and he wasn't even born in the Krays' day. What right has he to slag me off on his website? I think that the Twins had done about 20 years of their prison sentences when someone took Wraith on a visit to meet Reggie, just so he could say that he knew the Krays, which he never did. He even had the bloody cheek to say on his website: '*Branded By Ronnie Kray*, Lenny Hamilton. I cannot believe this book was published. Lenny is the man the media drag before the camera every time they want someone to slag the Krays off. He claims to have been branded by Ronnie Kray, hence the title. Forgive me for being a little cynical but wouldn't you have some sort of scar? I haven't met Lenny in the flesh... yet... but from seeing him on television I would say he is milking this. In my opinion it's a joke folks. But who am I to comment. Ideal for wedging in between the pipes in the toilet.'

Many people in the East End saw what Ronnie Kray did to me. When Harry Abrahams and Albert Donoghue saw the state I was in the next morning, they both went round to the Krays' house to find out why Ronnie did it. That's what you call good friends. Ronnie Kray told them to ask me to go and have a drink with him – and that's what you call a fucking maniac.

As for Steve Wraith – to say that I'm milking the system? Well, what would that Geordie idiot know? He should get in touch with the children's hospice in Liverpool, because that is where I sent some of the money that I was paid for appearing on television. I will agree with him that I do not have any visible scars. The reason for this is that I was told by two different doctors that I am one in so many thousands that have a rare type of healing skin. I was told that if I lived to be 90 my face would show no wrinkles. I guess they were right: I'm 75 now and I don't look it.

So, to prove what a first-class idiot Steve Wraith is I would like him to get in touch with Nipper Read, who cooperated with the writing of this book, because he will tell him that a top police doctor took photos of my face through some type of x-ray machine and it showed quite clearly the scars under the skin. If you still want to call me a liar, then put your money where your mouth is and pay for me to take a lie detector test.

It is people like Steve Wraith who watch films about the Twins and read books and talk about this which they have no first-hand knowledge of. If I was Steve Wraith I would keep my mouth shut.

In my opinion it was only the good policing of Mr Leonard 'Nipper' Read and his team after nearly two years of work that finally put a stop to the Kray twins' reign of terror in the East End. Do you know what that meant? It meant that people could walk into a pub and have a quiet drink again. People didn't need to look over their shoulder in fear of Ronnie Kray in one of his black moods.

As for myself, I openly confess that I was terrified of the Kray twins and only testified against them because they threatened my children. Any father would do the same for their kids.

I have been no angel, I admit that. I was a criminal from way back in the 1960s, working with the top professionals and nicking lorry loads of goods. I was taught to blow safes and finally went to work on my own. I became a jewel thief, but in all honesty I can say that I never robbed my own. As I sit here in my spotless flat in Bow, East London, and look back over all the years, I wonder how I could have done such things because I was always brought up by my father to be considerate to others.

I have seen criminals come and go, but the two men that I respect the most are Eric Mason and his son, Jeff. Don't forget that it was Eric who was nailed to the floor and brutalised by Frankie Fraser and the Richardson gang. Eric, as a consequence needed 305 stitches to close his wounds. It only took seven brave men to do that to him. Eric Mason has already written two very good books about his life in the underworld, and he also has a DVD [41], which I was privileged to take part in.

There is also my dear friend Billy Frost, who you have learned about in this book. He was one of the most trusted

LENNY HAMILTON WITH CRAIG CABELL

men on the Kray Firm. In fact, Frostie even lived with the Twins at one time in the 1960s, in a house in North London. Billy Frost stayed out of the limelight and was true to the Krays. He wasn't like the Krays, though. He was quite the opposite and it's true to say that not all of the people on the Kray Firm were bad men. Some of them even wanted to get away from the Krays, as I have already explained. But once you were on the Firm it was up to the Krays only whether you could stay or go.

As for me, when Ronnie saw that I didn't go to the police after he burnt me, I was asked if I would like to work for the Twins and be on the Firm. I told them: 'I have no disrespect to the both of you but I am happy as I am getting my own money.'

A lot of people have gone on TV and on the record to make a name for themselves regarding the Krays, but there is also a group of people who have stayed away from the limelight and told the truth whenever asked. I would like to include myself, Billy Frost, George and Alan Dixon and Eric Mason among those men. All, in some shape or form, have contributed to this book. It is up to the reader to form their own opinion about what we say.

Frankie Fraser has been less than truthful in the past. Fraser came from Camberwell, in South East London. He was on the Richardson Firm as one of their main henchmen. When the Krays were apparently going to war with the Richardsons, Ronnie put Fraser's name at the top of his hit list. The Krays hated Fraser, as a lot of people did. That's why he got the name The Poison Dwarf. As I stated, all I want is the truth to come out, but Fraser wouldn't know the truth if it hit him in the face. I know this because on one television programme he said that George Cornell and the Kray twins were great pals. That is a complete lie. I knew George and I knew that he hated their guts.

On another programme, Fraser said that he hit Eric Mason on the head with an axe. Well, he only did that once Eric was nailed to the floor. As Fraser swung his wonderful axe, Eric put his hand over his head and it split his hand in two. Furthermore, Fraser stated that he dumped Mason outside Whitechapel's London Hospital with the axe still in his head. This is another lie. Eddie Richardson said that Eric Mason was dumped outside Charing Cross Hospital, which was not far from where they carried out their evil deed. I believe Eddie Richardson of the two. Fraser tried to let people think that what he did to Eric was gallant and a single-handed affair, but he forgot to mention that he was team-handed. The truth – like many stories about the Krays – has been distorted over time.

There was also the time when Fraser cut Jack Spot, who was then known as the King of the Underworld. He was team-handed then as well, because Fraser didn't have the bottle to confront Spot on his own.

Freddie Foreman is a man I have respect for. Back in 2005 he confronted Fraser and knocked him out cold. But the brave Frankie Fraser never retaliated. Why? Because he has not got anyone to back him up today. The last time I saw Fraser was outside the Blind Beggar pub. I was with Billy Frost, who did time with Fraser in Pentonville Prison. They were both on Section Four together, before they both got transferred to Dartmoor Prison. In all, Billy Frost spent seven years in prison with Fraser and yet, when he stood next to him outside the Blind Beggar, Fraser made out that he did not know him. Billy Frost was once put on an identity parade with Fraser over the Spot incident and yet Fraser still couldn't identify Billy outside the Blind Beggar pub. Was it because he had hurt so many people that he was frightened that he might suffer some kind of revenge? While Billy and I were standing there I told Fraser that Eric Mason was inside the pub. Fraser said: 'What is he hiding from me for?' So I invited him inside to ask Eric himself. With that, he left. Another brave gangster! However, it was a good job Fraser never went inside because Eric Mason would have wiped the floor with him.

Frankie Fraser and Tony Lambrianou have said and written much, but they were compulsive liars who have lived off the Krays' name. Today, Fraser lives in North London, a far cry from his birthplace in Camberwell. Why is that? Was there some good reason for him to move from South London?

Tony Lambrianou really glorified in being thought of as one of the Kray henchmen. Long before he knew the Krays he was going about stealing car radios. That was the type of cheap thief he was. He was never a gangster. I call people like him Cardboard Gangsters. What did he know about the Krays? He was only on their Firm for less than two months. To me, his brother Chris is a real man. He openly admits that he was never a member of the Kray Firm.

Tony Lambrianou is a classic example of how a little television and press coverage, along with a book here and there, can make a small player in the Krays' world into a 'Kray Boss.'

I was on Nicky Campbell's television programme on 24

March 1995, which was called 'Should Reggie Kray Be Released From Prison?' I was approached about three weeks beforehand and was told who would be on the show, as was everyone else who was on it. I was then asked what I was going to say and my answer was that Reggie should never be released. About a week before I was to appear on the show, I started to get threatening phone calls, saying that I was to argue that Reggie should be released otherwise my partner and daughter would be seen to. I had no option but to cooperate with their demands. To me, Tony Lambrianou did not know what he was talking about on that show. He said that Jack McVitie 'challenged' the Twins, but couldn't elaborate any further as he didn't know what he was saying.

Tony Lambrianou then changed his story on another television programme. After the Twins were dead he said: 'I don't think they knew what they were doing.' He went on to ask if the Firm went down so that Reggie could write a book and confess to the more well-known killings. Why did he wait until Reggie was dead to say this? He never had the balls to do so when Reggie was alive.

Tony Lambrianou was a cheap thief and errand boy for the Twins. When Jack was alive, Tony was quite willing to accept free drinks off him, but after Jack's death all he could do was run his memory down. I want people to know that Tony Lambrianou wasn't fit to kiss Jack McVitie's arse.

JUST THROWING AWAY THE KEY

*'Everyone in London was talking about us.
It was getting to the point when either the police had
to break us or we would have broken them.'*

REGGIE KRAY

It was good that the authorities locked up the Krays and threw away the key. They hurt so many people. They didn't just duff them up, but cut them, maimed them and even killed them and disposed of the bodies. They were truly evil people.

And they didn't even care who they hurt: local people from their own community in the East End, innocent businessmen and traders, and even members of their own Firm that stayed loyal to them. The Krays didn't care about anybody but themselves.

I will happily take a lie-detector test to back up anything I've said here. Look at the people who are backing me up in this book: people from the East End, people who really knew the Krays. And then there is Nipper Read. We've all come together in order to tell the truth.

I want the public to know what goes on in the criminal world. You can take it from me that all the top criminals have got the police in their pockets, or they have somebody on the inside giving them information. Where there's enough money there are corrupt people. Take the screws in prison. Talking from personal experience, I know that if you had enough money they would bring into prison whatever you wanted. Not all of them were corrupt, of course, but enough were. There is no way that there would be such a big drugs problem in prisons today, for example, if the screws weren't helping to get the stuff in.

What is the world coming to?

What you have read is one of the most honest records of the Krays you are ever likely to come across. It's probably the scariest, too. Don't have nightmares, as they say on *Crimewatch*. Just leave those nightmares to the people who were there and had to suffer at the hands of the Kray twins – the people of my generation, not the youngsters who think they are Kray fans or would-be Krays. Those people don't know half of the truth, so how can they admire or imitate?

INTRODUCTORY
NOTE TO ANNEXES
BY CRAIG CABELL

Assisting Lenny Hamilton in putting this book together, it became clear to me that although much of what he states is first-hand information, certain readers would remain sceptical after reading Lenny's memories and perceptions. In order to add weight to his book, I conducted interviews with people who could authenticate or, at least back up, some of Lenny's reminiscences.

When Lenny says that he is relating 'the truth' and that he is prepared to undergo a lie-detector test to back up the claims he makes in this book, I believe him. But I believe him because I have had the benefit of sitting down with him many times to discuss his claims; the reader hasn't.

The interviews in this Annexe complement the book you

have just read and, I believe, add much weight to the revelations laid down. Only now is the truth about the Kray twins finally being revealed.

ANNEXE A
INTERVIEWS

LEONARD 'NIPPER' READ INTERVIEW

How did you choose the murders to charge the Krays with at the trial?

The answer to that is that we had three murders. Cornell, McVitie and Mitchell. Now legally a person is entitled to a separate trial for each murder so we had to find two that could be joined together in one trial. It was decided that there was a joinder between Cornell and McVitie because in each case it could be established that this was a leader of a criminal gang murdering someone in the presence of other people, conscious that those eye-witnesses would never give evidence against them because of the position they occupied as gang leaders. So, with Cornell, Ronnie could walk in to the pub full of people, shoot Cornell and walk out confident that no one would give evidence because of the position Ronnie occupied in the criminal underworld. So far as McVitie is concerned, Reggie held exactly the same position

187

and knew he could kill in the presence of witnesses whose silence could be assured because of who he was. So for those reasons these two cases were selected to be tried together with the reasoning that the Mitchell case would be tried on a separate occasion.

I thought the later date would be some considerable time later when the furore over the first Kray trial had died down but in fact there was only five weeks between them. This, I thought, was one of the reasons why we lost the Mitchell case but, on reflection, I suppose it would be difficult to find a jury who had not heard of the Kray case.

When Reggie Kray was on his death bed he admitted to one other murder. You were asked in a documentary who that could be and you said Teddy Smith.

There is nothing I know of that leads me to believe that the Krays killed Teddy Smith. There was a lot of rumour and speculation. But, nevertheless knowing that Reggie admitted to one more killing I would have thought that to be Teddy Smith. He was very close to them. He was the man who collected Mitchell from Dartmoor and wrote the letters for Mitchell to copy to the Home Office. It was Smith who got Mitchell to put his thumb print on the letters so he could be identified as the writer. Smith was very big with the Krays. He wrecked the Hideaway Club so that the owner could be persuaded to let them come in with him. He was a right hand man and suddenly he disappeared and no one knew where he had gone. At the time people within the gang element were giving me bits of evidence but nothing about Teddy. Donoghue was an example. He was charged with the murder of Mitchell and he sent his mother to see me at court asking me to go to see him straight away as he wanted to give me some information. I went to Brixton Prison where he told me the Krays' plan was that the case would be divided with Donoghue taking the blame for the Mitchell case and Ronnie Hart for the McVitie murder. Donoghue refused to accept this and threats were made that his wife and child would be assaulted.

He began to make a statement to me about the murder and I moved him from Brixton to Birmingham prison for his safety, and then I moved his wife and child to a safe house. Then we began to get the full story and started to look for the other people connected with the case. Some time later Ronnie Hart came forward to talk to me about the McVitie case but there was never a word about Teddy Smith. Nobody said a word to me about him. Nobody. All they said was 'Teddy's gone.' That's all.

Tell me about protecting the witnesses.
That side of the investigation caused me more trouble than anything else. It was all new you see. Nobody had never done anything like that before – especially on that scale – putting people in safe houses, hotels and so on and providing round the clock protection.

But how many people have done it since? Not many. It was such an intricate case with lots of people involved, huge media coverage?
It was very complex, and we were setting standards that other people would follow but they were standards that had never been heard of before. We had 248 people looking after the

witnesses! Imagine the people who were protesting against the scale of all that.

Did you ever encounter any professional jealousy?
Oh yes. I was assured that I would be the next Commander after the Kray case by the most senior officers at the Yard but it never happened of course... There was a lot of jealousy. It's perfectly normal in that sort of situation. In fact I had a sign in my office that read 'Success breeds many enemies' and I found that to be true.

Did you have a notice board with names on it, people who had been suspected of being murdered or who simply disappeared because of the Krays? I ask that because you have told me that there were other murders.
No. I was like the spider in the middle of the web. All the information was coming into me and I was the guy sitting in the middle of it all and I sifted the information and made notes to decide how we were going to investigate it. That's the way it was done. Nowadays, as you say, they have a big board and put all the names up, but I didn't do it that way.

All the witnesses I had were all scared out of their wits. But I told them I wouldn't call them as a witness until I had substantial evidence and, more importantly, until all the Kray gang were locked up. That was the only way I could get people on my side. They didn't even sign their statements when they were made, but later on, when we had more witnesses and substantial evidence, then they were signed.

You really looked after your witnesses, didn't you?
It was the only way. I remember sitting there in the Old Bailey when all those terrified people came up to give evidence and every one of them came up to expectation.

Did you come up with the idea of looking in the furnace under the swimming pool in Cheshire Street, in case they were burning bodies there or did Albert Donoghue suggest that to you?
No that was my idea. It was of no consequence at all. But there was an old man in charge there and the Krays used him as a post box. If they wanted anything sent to them they didn't want people to see they addressed it to him at the baths and then collected it later. The baths were exactly across the road from where they lived and I just thought it would be a convenient place to get rid of a body.

But what about the disposal of the bodies?
The Krays were probably responsible for putting round all kinds of misinformation about bodies propping up supermarkets and under motorways and such like to divert attention.

But you did dig up a farm in Kent?
Yes we did. We were told by a man serving time in Brixton prison that he knew where the bodies were buried. We got him out and he identified this farm as the location and we dug up acres of it. I was disgusted with the bloke who gave us the information but I suppose on reflection he could have easily have been a Kray plant.

But that's going down the same road as what Lenny is saying in his book – nearer the truth.
But what is the truth? Freddie Foreman talks of a trawler.

It's difficult finding evidence. It seems a lot of people were threatened by the Twins?
Donoghue told me that that the Krays got so paranoid towards the end that you couldn't live from day to day. They never knew who was going to be next. He said in the end they devised a kind of code. So if two guys came to the door and said 'We thought you was visiting your aunt in Cambridge', then the guy would know he was in trouble and disappear for a while.

How could they expect anyone to be loyal to them if they were considering bumping off their own Firm members?
Fear. Their loyalty was fear.

Lenny Hamilton was never a member of the Kray Firm, but how important was he to the case?
He was the first witness who I knew would give evidence against Ronnie Kray for a GBH case. A substantial case. And that was very important because up to that time all I had against them was fraud cases. Now don't let me disillusion you. The fraud cases were very solid cases most of which were supplied from information from Leslie Payne but I wanted far more serious cases to charge the Krays with. The problem was fear. You just can't believe the fear they generated. Let me try, if I can, to give you an example. Jack McVitie was murdered in the basement of a house. The woman who lived there was

known as Blonde Carol. So, as soon as the Krays were arrested
I had this woman brought to West End Central Police Station.
I told her that I knew all about the so-called party held there
but I wanted her to tell me who was there.

She asked me who I was talking about and I said the Krays.
She said 'Who? Never heard of them.' I rattled off the names
of some of the people who I knew were there and she still
denied it. Eventually I had her in that room for three hours,
but she said, 'No, no, no,' and so I had to let her go. Then when
we got the Mitchell murder charged I thought I would try
again at the McVitie case and I had her brought in again. And
she was still saying, 'No.' She was terrified. Absolutely
terrified. Even knowing that she was talking to a Detective
Superintendent in Scotland Yard's Murder Squad she was still
saying, 'No.'

The barmaid in the Blind Beggar was much the same. She
gave evidence under oath at the Inquest saying that she never
saw anything. She told me, 'Mr Read, I know what you think,
but I can't give evidence, it's more than my life's worth.' I
moved her to Essex, put her son in another school, had people
staying with her night and day.

This went on for months until one day she said, 'Mr Read,
I'm ready now.' And, when she got to the Old Bailey and was
accused of lying because she had given false evidence at the
Inquest, she agreed that she had and explained the fear she
was under.

So fear instilled their code of silence?
Yes that's absolutely right.

[The Interview with Nipper Read is important because it clearly shows that his investigation jigsaws into some of the findings of this book. Let us now discuss some of the findings with Lenny Hamilton and Billy Frost.]

LENNY HAMILTON AND BILLY FROST
INTERVIEW

Billy Frost: I used to be a good friend of Jack's. I liked Jack 'the Hat'.

Lenny Hamilton: He was my mate too.

BF: I saw him in the Farley [pub], you know the Farley?

LH: Yes.

BF: Well, I met him there... and he said to me 'They've had me over'. I asked who, and he said 'The Twins'. I asked how and he told me: 'We done a job in Union Road. Printing firm. We had about a quarter of a million quid's worth of gold in a security motor... some of it was powder but a lot of it was gold bars, but I'm going to fucking kill the Twins.' I said to him, 'Jack, if I was you, I'd wipe my fucking mouth, leave it at that.'

LH: They gave him three grand, didn't they?

BF: Four grand. He said that they had a grand each, four of them that helped out. They should have been on 30 or 40 grand... but Jack went and spoke out about it and signed his own death warrant. He went in the Regency with a gun in a holdall.

LH: Laurie O'Leary, a diamond of a man, said in his book that Jack went down there with a sawn-off shotgun, but he never. He went down there with an American service revolver that I bought for him at a party. He loved guns, didn't he? He used to have a little one in his waistcoat, didn't he?

BF: And then Lambrianou plied him with booze, took him around Carol's and that was the end of it.

BF: When it came to the Kray trial, Nipper Read thought I was dead. Because I had disappeared the same time as Teddy Smith the police thought I had been murdered along with Smith.

When they charged them with the murders I was gonna come up. Any of them who was in with that trial, they couldn't ask to see anyone. They had to put it in writing, stating if they wanted to see Nipper Read or whoever else on the case. Connie Whitehead wrote to Nipper Read and Read came in and Connie said: 'Look, they've killed Frostie.'

But I think Read sussed out that I wasn't dead because he was told. So nothing materialised, so I came in on the trot about nine years later.

I would have gone up to the Old Bailey. It would have helped them, wouldn't it? They had no body for Jack 'the Hat' McVitie, no body of Frank Mitchell, no Teddy Smith. The old Pole [Kapo] had all of them, didn't he?

LH: [to Craig Cabell] There you are.

CC: But what about Freddie Foreman's story of disposing of the bodies on a trawler at Newhaven?

BF: Rubbish, rubbish. He's not going to drop people in it.

CC: Wait a moment, the interesting thing here is that Nipper Read thought that the bodies were burned in the furnace under the swimming baths in Cheshire Street.

BF: They were burned.

CC: So Read was going down the right road then?

BF: Yeah, he was. I think they got a tip-off, because they went and dug up premises owned by a Kapo who got away from a concentration camp. He had an aluminium smelt and when the bodies turned up he used to freeze them up, then cut them up a bit at a time and put them in the smelt and they were gone.

I actually met the guy one day. I had to take an envelope to a pub called The World Turned Upside Down in the Old Kent Road. I went in and saw this big old bloke. I spoke to him, gave him the envelope, which obviously had money in, and he was gone.

They used to call him The Undertaker. I can't remember his name. It was Polish. But then again, I don't think even the name he used was a real one.

[The discussion then moved on to other murders]

BF: I know they killed Georgie Francis.

CC: Who was he?

BF: He was a grass. He wasn't on the Firm.

LH: I knew Georgie Francis. Harry Abrahams upped him [punched him].

BF: Francis apparently did a lot of damage to Freddie Foreman's Firm.

CC: So did they get rid of him as a favour to Foreman?

BF: Well, he upset other people as well.

CC: But he just disappeared one day?

BF: That's right.

[A discussion of the Twins and their charity handouts]

CC: Would you say that the Twins ever helped you?

BF: They never helped no one.

LH: They helped themselves.

BF: They could be very kind in some ways. I've seen them pay people's rent.

LH: They used to give old people a pound or two, but it wasn't their money, was it?

BF: I first met the Twins over the Royal in Tottenham, back in the 1950s. Ronnie got his first conviction there when he chained a geezer. The chain came from a machine, one end of it was like a razor and Ronnie really hammered the geezer with one of them. But then chains weren't enough. They got their guns from Waterman. I liked him.

LH: Yeah, he was a nice guy.

BF: He had a lovely place. A mansion out in Surrey somewhere. He had money. He would kill anyone for a price. I think he wanted to be an assassin.

[Billy discusses the Twins banter with Lenny]

BF: I lived with the Twins for a while and I used to hear them having a go at each other. Ronnie would say, 'Don't do things after you get fuckin' pissed, getting plenty of Dutch courage down ya. Do what I did in the early evening, doing what you have to do.'

Ronnie never really took a liberty with people. With Ronnie, if you did something wrong, he'd come after you. He was as straightforward as that.

LH: I remember when some Scotch people were calling Big Pat Connolly a grass. He got on a plane and went up to Scotland by himself to sort it out.

BF: You had to behave yourself on the Firm. If you went out and started harassing somebody – misbehaving – the Twins would pull you up.

LH: When Teddy Smith, a lovely fella, got drunk you wanted to get miles away from him. Because he used to smash things up, people got to think that the Krays couldn't control their own Firm. That's why they had the needle with him.

BF: Ronnie was a man of whims. If he was nice in the morning, by 6:00 p.m. at night he'd be an arsehole. He had to start on someone. Connie Whitehead was scared of him. Ronnie said of himself: 'If anyone isn't scared of me they've got to be mad'.

LH: The only one who could control him was his mother. Nobody else, not even Charlie.

BF: They stopped Charlie's money once – his pension, as they called it. And Charlie, to show it didn't bother him, went out and bought himself some new clothes.

LH: The trouble with the Twins was that they were hated. Well, they were feared. But Charlie, their brother, was respected, and they couldn't get to the bottom of it. They didn't understand how people liked Charlie and not them. Then they got the hump. Charlie never hurt anyone. You can't put him down for what his brothers did.

BF: Reggie was a cold man. Very *cold*. Softly spoken. So much so, you had to really strain to hear him sometimes. You never really knew what he was thinking. Ronnie, you could understand.

WRITING ABOUT THE KRAYS

'I thought then about my own family and the Twins.
My mother, Rose, had known them since they were kids
visiting our rented Victorian house in Cheshire Street, around
the corner from their home in Vallance Road. When I told
her of their frequent troubles and their being arrested, she
would reply, "Why don't they leave the poor little sods
alone?" I had to remind her that they weren't poor
little sods, but that is how she saw them. In her eyes
it was always "The others who must have caused it".'
RONNIE KRAY – *A MAN AMONGST MEN*, BY LAURIE O' LEARY

The problem with writing about the Kray twins is that there are so many books out there. Any publisher, let alone punter, will ask – quite legitimately – 'What is there left to say?'

The answer: a true insight.

Like any true story there is good, bad, funny and sad. The

story of the Kray twins is no exception. It takes in all the emotions. One minute, they are branding someone with red-hot pokers, the next Ronnie is taking umbrage to a little caged bird singing: 'Ronnie is a gangster.' Extreme terror to knockabout comedy, their story has it all.

Laurie O'Leary was a lifelong friend of Ronnie Kray and his book reflected this with humour and poignancy. One thing he wanted to point out was that Ronnie Kray had a good sense of humour. Others have said this, too. Of course, Ronnie Kray was mentally unwell at certain times of his life and Laurie understood that as well. In fact, Laurie didn't flinch from anything in telling his story. That is why his book about Ronnie Kray is one of the best ever written.

The twins wrote their own books. But they wrote while in captivity. Consequently, their stories were compromised. Reggie's last book contained a message to the younger generation not to become gangsters. But did he mean it, or was it just his way of showing remorse in order to get the parole he wanted before the cancer got to him? That is the million-dollar question. The irony is that this last message became his legacy. The book was published after his death and showed Reggie in defeat, urging people not to follow his example. This was not the Reggie that many people in the East End remember. They saw the true man, a man who was cold, cruel and calculating. Look at the classic black-and-white photo of Reggie with the fag dangling from his mouth, look at his eyes. They say a picture paints a thousand words, and they are right.

Indeed, many people say that Reggie Kray was the more

evil one. Ronnie was unwell, so we can understand – to a degree – where his badness came from. Reggie didn't have this same excuse. Also, Ronnie could be very generous and funny.

The trouble with the Twins is that many people were all too willing to glamorise them and their acts. We've all seen the pictures of them hob-nobbing with celebrities, or the designer crime photos of the Twins staring menacingly at the camera or strutting down the street and holding court at Fort Vallance. These photographs have left an image of the Twins in the public's mind that is hard to knock down.

The Krays were masters of image control. Spin we'd call it today. They wanted themselves portrayed in a certain way and they got what they wanted. People will always be fascinated by tough, good-looking young men operating on the fringes of society. The Krays knew this instinctively and played up to the image that society had of them. They made sure that they always looked right, suited and booted at all times, and played the part of hard-but-fair men of the people. The public at large lapped it up then and they still do now. Yet, as this book clearly shows, the Krays do not deserve this perpetual celebrity image. They were wicked men. So long as books keep coming out about them – true or false – the myth, the legend, will continue despite the truth. All we can say about this book is that those of us who have collaborated on it believe it to be one of the most truthful books about the Twins.

It seems that the general public has a passion for the macabre, whether it's the Krays, Jack the Ripper or even the Nazis. That will never end, so all some of us can do is lay out

the truth as we see it before the public and hope that the
evidence is enough for them to think again how they see the
Krays. That's *why* you need the perceptions of the people who
were there — the people who experienced the very real
violence and pain that the Twins inflicted, or who saw
Ronnie Kray with his false teeth out and his hair unkempt.
These images of the Krays are just as real — more real, in
fact — than the stage-managed photographs that they liked to
put out for public consumption.

WOULD-BE KRAYS

As the Kray legend is such a powerful and long-lasting one it is no surprise that each generation since the time of the Twins has been attracted by the glitz, glamour, danger, power and mystique of designer crime. There has been no shortage of would-be Krays, prepared to unquestioningly accept the Kray myth. But, as both Nipper Read and Laurie O'Leary say: Why believe the words of a killer serving life in prison?

What is glamorous and exciting about the story of two men who spent half of their lives behind bars? What, in this story, is worth emulating?

The Twins' story started in the boxing ring and then spilled out onto the streets that they grew up on. Gang warfare then ensued, with knives, swords, chains and eventually guns coming into play. To the ill-informed, this all looks terribly exciting. But the reality is less so. Look at the shooting of George Cornell. Here we see a paranoid schizophrenic getting excited in the Blind Beggar pub, pulling a gun and shooting madly. This was not the calm killer of popular legend at work.

Today, crime is different. Life seems to be much cheaper and there are remorseless killers working the streets. This also ties into the myth of the Krays, as people look back to what they see as a simpler age, where the line between criminals and civilians was more clearly defined. But we know that's not true either. The Krays did not just harm their own kind. Anyone was fair game to the Twins, if there was any money in it for them.

There is simply no point in idolising or glamorising the Krays. They were just a couple of gangsters who got caught.

ANNEXE D

THE KRAYS' VICTIMS

Victim	Killed by
Billy Bannister	Reggie Kray
George Cornell	Ronnie Kray
Georgie Frances	the Kray twins
Frank Mitchell	on request of Ronnie Kray
The Rent Boy (name not known)	Ronnie Kray
Jack McVitie	Reggie Kray
Brian Scully	Reggie Kray
Frances Shea	driven to suicide by Krays
Teddy Smith	Reggie Kray
The Bank Manager	driven to suicide by ex-Firm members

ODE TO THE KRAYS
BY LENNY HAMILTON

Gone now are those wicked twins,
Laid to rest for their evil sins,
Yes it's true they were both gay,
Reggie and Ronnie Kray.

They cut and carved their names to fame,
Causing people so much pain,
Using people along the way,
It was them, those Twins called Kray.

Brother Charlie was a good man,
I thought that he was nice,
Because of his mad brothers,
He had to pay the price.

GETTING AWAY WITH MURDER

Charlie Kray and Freddie Foreman,
Received ten years in jail each,
For disposing of Jack the Hat's body,
While police were out of reach.

Jack the Hat was a good friend of mine,
Not as bad as the Twins said,
He was taken to Blonde Carol's house,
Where Reggie stabbed Jack to death.

Frank Mitchell the gentle giant,
They had him sprung from jail,
He trusted them with his life,
But to no avail.

They hid Frank in a house in Barking Road,
Frank was a nice and genuine geezer,
A girl they got for him,
Who went by the name of Lisa.

Frank got too much to handle,
The Krays could not control him,
So they had him taken outside and murdered,
On the orders of the brothers grim.

George Cornell, I worked for him,
Down in Billingsgate,
He was shot dead in the Blind Beggar pub,
By Ronnie Kray who decided his fate.

Cornell was a very hard man,
He knew Ronnie Kray was gay,
And he did call him a 'big fat poof',
In the Astor Club one day.

So many lies have been said,
About those brothers Kray,
And now that they are all dead,
Their myth lives on today.

They brought about their own downfall,
Because of all their greed,
Let's not forget they were murderers,
Never, ever to be freed.

Reggie Kray was in love with Frankie Shea,
But Frankie was having none of him,
So Frankie had it far away,
Far from the brother grim.

Reggie Kray was Frances' childhood sweetheart,
So the papers say,
So many lies have come about,
Because of the brothers Kray.

Reggie Kray he was bisexual,
He took Frances for his wife,
How he treated that poor sweet girl,
Made her take her own life.

So let's not forget poor Frances,
She was living in a life of fear,
Because of that evil Reggie Kray,
Frances paid so dear.

Let's not feel sorry for Reggie Kray,
Because he liked boys as well,
If Frances was alive today,
What a story she could tell.

Reggie and Ronnie have gone now,
For they have committed many a sin,
As for me I say good riddance,
To those evil brothers grim.

So listen all you young people out there,
And please listen to what I say,
Don't go down that wicked road,
Of those brothers Kray.

LIVING WITH FEAR

A brick mid-winter with the ice and snow,
Home fires burning but no direction home,
Got some work to do for those brothers of mine,
Feels like I've got a yellow stripe running down my spine.

Chorus:
But my wife is safe, the children as well,
But everything else is a living hell,
Going to the bar for a pint of beer,
Is a big thing to do when you're living with fear.

My brothers are standing up at the bar,
And there are plenty of people who carry their scars,
Nobody wants to laugh or make a sound,
'Cause suddenly it may be their turn around.

(repeat chorus)

GETTING AWAY WITH MURDER

The fear is so big, so deep, so long,
And how everyone wishes that my brothers were gone,
But when they're so much a part of your life,
You really don't know which way to turn.

© Johnnie Harvest. Lyrics used by permission

[These song lyrics were written about Charlie Kray and his perceived relationship with his brothers.]

DUST TO DUST

*'Not riches makes a king... A king is he that
hath laid fear aside.'*
SENECA

If you walk the East End streets today you will see plush new
developments everywhere. Years ago, Wapping was one of
the poorest areas of London. The Irish settled there originally
and built little hamlets to live in. Today that squalor has been
turned into luxury apartments and office blocks. You'd be
lucky to buy anything under £250,000. The East End is a real
rags to riches story.

The whole attitude of the East End has changed, not just
because of these new developments but also as a result of
higher standards of living – for most – and further racial
integration. Gone are the days when you could have a good
old knees-up in the many public houses that were a major
part of East End society.

My memories of such things haven't changed, though. I turn
again to the old docks. I recall the long sheds where both

produce and hardware were stored when the Thames was alive with ships. I think of the many vans and lorries that used to deliver the goods to all parts of the country. This was the old world that I knew, and that the Krays knew, too. It was cockney London, a world detached from the ruthless, drug-crazed urbanites of today, a world where you did the right thing for your neighbour, family and friends. Yes, the Krays knew this world and sometimes they participated in it. But they always had their own agenda. They were detached from that society. They robbed, killed and maimed and society eventually decided that it would exclude the Krays from it for the rest of their lives.

Now they are gone and the full truth has been told. Not just through this book and the authors' previous books but the books by Laurie O'Leary, Eric Mason and Nipper Read as well. Oddly, if you read the first edition of Charlie Kray's book – if you can find one – you'll see that he tells an interesting story, too, which authenticates some of the findings in this and the other books mentioned.

So let it rest. The story has been told by the people who were there. The jury has cast judgement, the keys thrown away. The killers are now dead and answering to a higher authority. The people who were left behind – some maimed or disfigured – have picked up the pieces of their lives. They have spoken and I believe that the final conclusion has been reached: the Kray Twins were cold-hearted murderers with no glamour attached to them at all.

Ashes to ashes, dust to dust. And good riddance to the pair of them.

Lenny Hamilton
Bow, 2006

BIBLIOGRAPHY

Foreman, Freddie, *Respect*, Century, 1996.

Foreman, Freddie, and Lambrianou, Tony, with Clerk, Carol, *Getting It Straight – Villains Talking*, Sidgwick & Jackson, 2001.

Kray, Charlie, with McGibbon, Robin, *Me And My Brothers*, HarperCollins, 1997.

Kray, Charlie, with Fry, Colin, *Doing the Business – The Deathbed Confessions*, Blake Publishing, 2001.

Kray, Reg, with Clerk, Carol, *A Way Of Life – Over Thirty Years Of Blood, Sweat And Tears*, Sidgwick & Jackson, 2000.

Kray, Reg, with Clerk, Carol, *Born Fighter*, Century, 1990.

Kray, Reg, *Thoughts, Philosophy And Poetry*, River Publishing, 1991.

Kray, Reg and Ron, with Dinenage, Fred, *Our Story*, Sidgwick & Jackson, 1988.

Kray, Ron, with Dinenage, Fred, *My Story*, Sidgwick & Jackson, 1993.

Lambrianou, Chris, *Escape – From The Kray Madness*, Sidgwick & Jackson, 1995.

Lambrianou, Tony, *Inside The Firm*, Smith Gryphon Ltd, 1991.

O' Leary, Laurie, *Ronnie Kray – A Man Amongst Men*, Headline, 2001.

Pearson, John, *The Profession Of Violence*, HarperCollins, 1995.

Pearson, John, *The Cult Of Violence*, Orion, 2001.

Read, Leonard, with Morton, James, *Nipper Read – The Man Who Nicked The Krays*, Little Brown, 2001.

SOURCE DOCUMENTATION

Certain documents were studied for this book, mainly pertaining to the murder charges the Krays were actually tried for in 1969. National Archive records used as source documentation to support this book are as follows:

CRIM 1/2064, CRIM 1/2747, CRIM 1/3142, CRIM 1/4900, CRIM 1/4901, CRIM 1/4902, CRIM 1/4903, CRIM 1/404, CRIM 1/4905, CRIM 1/4906, CRIM 1/4907, CRIM 1/4908, CRIM 1/4909, CRIM 1/4910, CRIM 1/4927, CRIM 1/4942, CRIM 1/4943, CRIM 1/4944, CRIM 1/4945, CRIM 1/4946, CRIM 1/4947, CRIM 1/4948, CRIM 1/4949, CRIM 1/4990, CRIM 1/4991, CRIM 1/4992, CRIM 1/5006, CRIM 1/5007, CRIM 1/5008, CRIM 1/5009, CRIM 1/5010, CRIM 1/5044, CRIM 1/5045, CRIM 1/5125, CRIM 1/5126, CRIM 1/5127, CRIM 1/5128, CRIM 1/5129, CRIM 1/5131.

DPP 2/4510, DPP 2/4511, DPP 2/4512, DPP 2/4513, DPP 2/4514, DPP 2/4515, DPP 2/4516, DPP 2/4517, DPP 2/4518, DPP 2/4519, DPP 2/4520, DPP 2/4521, DPP 2/4522, DPP 2/4523, DPP 2/4524, DPP 2/4525, DPP 2/4527, DPP 2/4528, DPP 2/4529.

CO 852/2446, CO 968/12/8, CO 968/900, CO 968/902, CO 1015/2645, CO 1032/510. CO 1036/1643, CO 1037/256, CO 1067/8.

DO 121/86, DO 154/98, DO 194/62, DO 194/73.

FCO 12/63, FO 778/40, FO 1117/4.

Other documents were used for information purposes only and are credited either in the text for authenticity or by end note where applicable.

SUPPORTING INTERVIEWS

Leonard 'Nipper' Read interview, May 2006.
Lenny Hamilton and Billy Frost Interview, October 2005.

GLOSSARY OF TERMS

Bent	Corrupt policeman or stolen goods
Blags	Robbing security vans
Chokey	Solitary confinement
Doing Bird	Spending time in prison
Firm	A gang of criminals
Frighteners	Scare somebody into doing something
Gaff	Somebody's home
Grass	A person who informs the police
Manor	An area where somebody lives
Nick	Prison
Screw	A prison officer
Shooter	Gun
Slag off	Putting someone down
Spiel (Spieler)	Unlicensed gambling club
Stretch	Prison sentence
Tickle	Robbery
Tom	Jewellery (i.e., Tom Foolery)
Tool	Weapon

Touch	Money made from ill-gotten gains
Trot	Go AWOL (Absent Without Leave)
Upped	Beat up in a fight

COPYRIGHT

ABOUT THE AUTHORS

Lenny Hamilton is a former jewel thief who worked for Harry Abrahams' Firm during the 1960s. He was later branded with red-hot pokers by Ronnie Kray late one night in the Krays' nightclub, Esmeralda's Barn. Lenny is the writer of one previous book, *Branded By Ronnie Kray*, and still lives in the East End today.

Craig Cabell is the writer of ten books, including *The Kray Brothers – The Image Shattered* and *James Herbert – Devil In The Dark*. He has also edited and written special Forewords to several military history books. He has been a freelance writer for more than 15 years, working most notably for *The Independent* and as an in-house reporter for *MOD Focus*.

FOOTNOTES

1) Not Stene Street, as mentioned by John Pearson in his books, or even the Twins in their books. Charlie Kray spells it correctly in his book and the name can be easily looked up today on any street map.

2) According to *Our Story*, the Twins' joint autobiography (which is slightly different in its hardback and paperback versions), Reggie and Ronnie were called up into the army in the spring of 1952, which means they were on the run from the service in 1952 and 1953.

3) Charlie Kray maintained until his death that they should have stayed in the army and become physical training instructors. They were exceptional boxers at that time, still very capable and very fit. He explained in *The Image Shattered* that it would have been a 'different world' if they had kept up the boxing, and many people agree with that. But as Ronnie admits in *Our Story*, he started to become unwell while in Shepton Mallet (page 25 in the original hardback version of *Our Story*).

4) This was in 1954.

5) This story is a good example of where the movie *The Krays* glamorised the story of the Twins. The truth as laid down in this book shows a more gritty realism, which I'm afraid destroys the 'designer crime' image.

6) According to Ronnie Kray's criminal record he was sent down for three years on 5 November 1956 for 'Wounding with intent and possession of an offensive weapon'. In *Our Story* Reggie Kray mentions that he opened the Double R Club with brother Charlie in 1959 (page 34 of the first edition). This would be towards the end of Ronnie's sentence.

7) Reggie and Charlie, still keen on boxing, set up a gym above the club, which they got Henry Cooper to open. The Double R Club was the beginning of their celebrity days.

8) It must be appreciated that before going into prison Ronnie had shot his first man. Also, he had to be put in a padded cell whilst in Camp Hill Prison on the Isle of Wight when, by his own admission, he really lost it (see his autobiography *My Story*) when he was told matter-of-factly by a prison warder that his favourite aunt, Rose, had died. This didn't happen while Reggie was on his honeymoon as depicted in the movie *The Krays*; she died while Ronnie was serving his three-year prison sentence!

9) This has been said by Laurie O'Leary and Tony Lambrianou in the past; in the book and *The Kray Brothers – The Image Shattered*.

10) At 9:15 a.m. on Wednesday, 6 January 1965, Nipper Read and Fred Gerrard arrested the Twins in the basement bar of the Glenrae Hotel in Seven Sisters for demanding money with menaces. On 7 January (PRO reference MEPO2/10763, also in *The Guardian*, 8 January 1965), the Twins were charged with

demanding money with menaces at Old Street magistrates court and remanded in custody until 15 January. On 1 February the Krays applied for bail. This was refused on 8 February. An appeal was lodged on 10 February but dismissed on 12 February. Lord Boothby then asked in the House of Lords whether 'it is the intention to imprison the Kray brothers indefinitely without trial?' On 28 February the trial was announced and on 9 March the Twins were brought to court. After a ten-day hearing (ending on 18 March), the jury retired for three and a half hours. On their return the foreman announced that they couldn't reach a verdict. They were advised to go away for another half an hour. They did so but still failed to reach a verdict. There was no majority decision in those days, the verdict had to be unanimous. A re-trial was ordered to start on 30 March.

11) This theory doesn't hang together because a second photo within the sequence shows Boothby sharing a joke with Teddy Smith, which suggests somebody else was taking the photos. The answer: another known homosexual, Leslie Holt, who appeared in a third photograph. So, Smith and Holt took the photos.

12) See National Archive record MEPO 2/10763.

13) See Chapter Nine 'The Peer and the Gangster', *The Cult Of Violence* (Orion, 2001), by John Pearson for his perceptions based upon official records and first-hand accounts.

14) See *The Cult Of Violence* by John Pearson, as above.

15) See Leonard 'Nipper' Read interview in *The Kray Brothers – The Image Shattered*, Robson, 2002.

16) This particular scene is documented in National Archive reference CRIM 1/5128 (original transcriptions made by George Walpole & Co., official shorthand writers to the CCC);

GETTING AWAY WITH MURDER

also an edited transcript can be found at Annexe B 'trial Transcript' in *The Kray Brothers – The Image Shattered*.

17) Interestingly, the original *Express* cartoon of this 'fat slob' outburst was used in the photo section to the first edition of Charlie Kray's book *Me And My Brothers* (Everest Books Limited, 1976), along with another cartoon. Released shortly after he came out of prison, Charlie admitted that the original version of his book was written in bad blood against his brothers. However, it is an important document for criminologists today.

18) Charlie Kray interview with Craig Cabell, *Midweek* magazine, 1995.

19) See interviews in Annexe for first-hand opinions connected with the Kray trial from Kray associates.

20) See CRIM 1/4916 Part B at the National Archive.

21) It must be fully appreciated that Ronnie Kray was certified insane. People try to rationalise his actions, but you cannot rationalise the ways of a mad man. One minute he was alright, the next he was carving people up. People simply have to accept that he was completely unpredictable.

22) When this chapter was discussed with Nipper Read and the two hand guns shot by Ronnie Kray theory put to him, he stated that Ronnie didn't have two guns. Ian Barrie had the other and fired it to clear the area. In the past it has been said that Barrie had a shotgun. However, Donoghue never mentions a shotgun being passed for disposal, which suggests that if Barrie took one he never fired it.

23) This conversation is taken from the narrative of the trial as detailed in the source documentation (see credits) in the National Archive.

232

24) This is the spelling of the gentleman's name as stated in records at the National Archive.

25) The wound at the back of Cornell's head is the exit wound of the bullet; photos of the entrance and exit wounds can be found at the National Archive.

26) Tony Barry has confirmed this on TV documentaries dedicated to the Kray twins' tyranny.

27) He didn't try to escape and go head-first through the glass as mentioned by some people and as portrayed in the movie *The Krays*.

28) When John Pearson first met the Krays, shortly after the McVitie murder (see *The Cult Of Violence*), he stated that Reggie's hand was bandaged.

29) I can understand the logic here as the covert helper was known as the 'Undertaker', but he wasn't one.

30) It has been said that if somebody inside prison needed to be taught a lesson and that person unfortunately happened to be in Mitchell's prison, then the big man would put on the frighteners for the Twins. He would get some money for it, but more importantly, the Twins – probably Ronnie – promised him a release date (i.e., that they would get him out).

31) Albert Donoghue and Teddy Smith.

32) Albert Donoghue has stated that when Frank got into the car he pulled out a large knife and started threatening the Firm members. This was because he partly believed that they had been sent to kill him. But why? Albert Donoghue has stated that the Twins used to write letters to Mitchell while he was inside. Obviously, he would pass these letters around, thus proving his friendship with the Krays and enforcing his claim

that they were not men of their word and that they weren't getting him out. So, was springing Mitchell a PR exercise?

33) Frank Mitchell escaped on 12 December 1966 and met his end on 23 December 1966.

34) The Krays had a dilemma. They didn't want an irate Mitchell on their doorstep. Despite their power and influence, they couldn't contain a desperate and fuming giant such as Mitchell. Also, Mitchell's reputation was almost as fearsome as theirs. Something had to be done about the Mitchell embarrassment. Ronnie apparently made the final decision. He knew Mitchell. He was the one who had started the friendship with the man and he was the one who would have to end it. Mitchell had to go. Enter Freddie Foreman and Alfie Gerrard.

35) Craig Cabell interview with Nipper Read, 2001.

36) This was mainly because Reggie spent two short terms in prison, for the Daniel Shay and Hugh McCowan incidents.

37) This is detailed in many books about the Krays, not least the ones written by themselves. However, for a sensitive analysis of Ronnie Kray's state of mind see *Ronnie Kray – A Man Amongst Men* by Laurie O'Leary.

38) Quote taken from the Third Edition hardback 1984.

39) This story lends support to the idea of Ronnie Kray having two guns on him in the Blind Beggar the night he killed George Cornell.

40) Nipper Read was interviewed for an Annexe of this book. During the interview he was asked about the other names he investigated as part of the Kray murder case, but time has washed away those memories unfortunately.

41) Entitled *The Last Man Standing*.